GEORGE A. LARSON · JAY PRIDMORE

CHICAGO ARCHITECTURE AND DESIGN

WITH PHOTOGRAPHY BY HEDRICH-BLESSING

HARRY N. ABRAMS, INC. · PUBLISHERS

TO SUSAN AND KIM WITH DEEP APPRECIATION FOR THEIR CONTINUED SUPPORT

PROJECT MANAGER: LETA BOSTELMAN

EDITOR: JOAN E. FISHER

DESIGNER: JUDITH MICHAEL

Half title page: Front door of Glessner House, 1887, H. H. Richardson
Title page: United Airlines Terminal, O'Hare International Airport, 1987, Murphy/Jahn
Contents page: Fountain (dismantled) by Louis Comfort Tiffany, Congress Hotel, 1883, Holabird and Roche
Page six: 181 West Madison Street, 1990, Cesar Pelli and Associates
Page eight: Ornament detail from Carson Pirie Scott exterior, 1904, Louis H. Sullivan
Page ten: Children's playroom in Frank Lloyd Wright Home and Studio, Oak Park, 1889–1909, Frank Lloyd Wright
Pages twelve and thirteen: Farnsworth House, Plano, 1951, Ludwig Mies van der Rohe

LIBRARY OF CONGRESS CATALOGING-IN-PUBLICATION DATA

Larson, George A.
Chicago architecture and design / by George A. Larson and Jay Pridmore ;
with photography by Hedrich-Blessing.
p.   cm.
Includes bibliographical references and index.
ISBN 0-8109-3192-3
1. Architecture—Illinois—Chicago.   2. Architecture, Modern—19th
century—Illinois—Chicago.   3. Architecture, Modern—20th century—
Illinois—Chicago.   4. Chicago (Ill.)—Buildings, structures, etc.
I. Title.
NA735.C4L37   1993
720'.9773'11—dc20   93–18306
                         CIP

CONTENTS

For an architect, Chicago is *the* American city. Its name conjures a mythical place where its architects were larger than life, and its buildings were new and noble. I have visited Chicago many times; I have even designed for Chicago, but this has not affected my image of this ideal city or its special position in my heart.

Revisiting in my mind the spatial and temporal limits of that mythical place, I see them as extremely compact. The Great Chicago Fire of 1871 provoked this architectural explosion, which in our terms actually began in 1884 with the construction of the Home Insurance Building (the first skyscraper?) by William Le Baron Jenney and ended in 1893 with the World's Columbian Exposition. This is the critical period, although we may extend it to start in 1882 with the Montauk Building by Burnham and Root and close in 1899 with the Schlesinger-Mayer (later Carson Pirie Scott) store by Louis Sullivan.

This was the period that produced several great architects and created (apparently out of nothing) a new and very American vision of architecture. It was one of the earliest and strongest waves of modernity and was the first time that an American architecture led the world. This was when its architects were at ease combining poetry with pragmatism. It was not only a short time span, but it was also a well-defined place: the Loop. Here is where all the great buildings happened, including the Rookery, the Tacoma, the Reliance, the Gage, and the Monadnock (that most impure masterpiece). In addition, this wave of architectural wonders was comprised of almost one single building type: the tall office building.

There were two dominant architectural figures, John Wellborn Root and Louis Sullivan, as well as several very good architects, such as Holabird and Roche. I have particular admiration and respect for these great, tough, pragmatic artists. They were not put off by their difficult and very limited problems. On the contrary, they seem to have relished them, designing great buildings in a straightforward but lyrical way and with an incredible creative force that in a few years forever changed the limits and possibilities of what we call Architecture.

Great architecture in Chicago did not end with Root and Sullivan. They were followed by a number of other great architects, most notably Frank Lloyd Wright and Mies van der Rohe. They and others have contributed much to the continuing architectural strength of Chicago even though they were not part of its mythical moment when a new urban architecture was first created.

A city is a living thing and as such is always changing. It is up to those who build its buildings and set the parameters for its growth to make it into a healthy and rich organism. Because it is living, it will always be open to new interpretations. We shall never have a final word on it—at best only an increased understanding. *Chicago Architecture and Design* is a welcome and insightful contribution to our understanding of the history of Chicago's architecture and its architects.

Cesar Pelli
Cesar Pelli & Associates

When people remember a building, it is often their impression of its interior spaces that remains in focus rather than what was significant about the exterior. So it is surprising that there have been many books about the architecture of Chicago, but never one that would emphasize the significant interiors.

In the summer of 1951, at the age of sixteen, I discovered a new building that made an indelible and lasting impression on me. This revolutionary building was 860 Lake Shore Drive, designed by Mies van der Rohe, and it would change the course of my life.

As I experienced the excitement of driving on Lake Shore Drive, with the views of the approaching city and the trembling lights of the shoreline buildings, I decided then that this would be where I would live, leaving Detroit, which I considered to be a city without architectural inspiration other than the Cranbrook school by Eliel Saarinen.

Chicago is the city I came to the day after my graduation from the College of Architecture and Design at the University of Michigan in 1957. Through my father's introduction to Ralph Eckerstrom, then director of design at the Container Corporation of America, I was hired by Skidmore, Owings and Merrill to begin a career in architecture and design. This was the golden age of SOM. In the new Inland Steel Building designed by SOM, I was immersed in the most innovative planning and preeminent interiors of our time, including commissions by Calder, Lippold, Bertoia, and Seymour Lipton. It was here that I learned the real principles of architecture and the philosophy of planning and designing a building from the inside out.

In 1959 I went to C. F. Murphy Associates and then back to SOM, and in 1978 I left to establish my own firm with my partner and wife, Susan Larson. Our partnership began with the planning of our own home in Evanston and grew to include such major corporate institutions of Chicago as the Sara Lee Corporation, John Nuveen and Company, and Aon Corporation. Ironically, I returned to Detroit in the eighties to design projects for General Motors and the Ford Company. Today we have expanded our roster to include residential projects as well. Although our focus was at first on interiors, we now provide architectural services as well.

My belief has always been that there is no difference between architecture and interiors; one drives the other. They are in fact one statement. Architects do not design in a vacuum. Architecture is about problem solving; it requires creative, formal interaction with the historical, economic, cultural, and psychological requirements of each project.

Chicago is one of the most exciting cities in the world for architecture and design. Here is where the story of twentieth-century architecture happened, where the icon of our business world began with the first skyscraper. Here is where Frank Lloyd Wright designed furniture, carpets, textiles, china, and glass walls to complete the design of his projects.

This book is a chronological story beginning in 1887 with the Glessner House and bringing us to today. As the story unfolds, we view Chicago's unique structures and see what it is that ties these projects together and makes buildings and spaces memorable and lasting. We will speak of space, proportions, lighting, juxtaposition of materials, and the integration of form following function. We try to bring alive Chicago's wonderful architectural heritage and to help readers everywhere understand the principles that have made this the most important architectural city of the twentieth century.

Chicago Architecture and Design is filled with beautiful photographs from the collection of Hedrich-Blessing of Chicago. Jack Hedrich is a longtime friend who agreed to our use of these photographs before they were given to the Chicago Historical Society. This book would not have been possible without his generous contribution. Hedrich-Blessing began its business in 1929 and continues today, documenting significant works that contain the best architectural traditions in Chicago. I am very grateful for Hedrich-Blessing's participation, which brings to light many unpublished works of real significance.

The real inspiration for this book has been the genius and creativity of the dedicated architects and designers who are represented in these pages. It is their ingenious yet simple and direct solutions to the problems of space and their articulation of the architecture that have left Chicago with such an enduring legacy.

George A. Larson
Larson Associates

ACKNOWLEDGMENTS

One of the great pleasures in assembling and writing this book was the opportunity to see Chicago architecture through the eyes of the people who have devoted their lives and careers to it. Their knowledge and assistance were indispensable in our efforts.

Among those we interviewed in our research were architects Thomas Beeby, Larry Booth, Jacques Brownson, George Danforth, Joseph Fujikawa, Myron Goldsmith, Wilbert Hasbrouck, John Holabird Jr., Thomas Harboe, Gerald Horne, Paul Janicki, Dirk Lohan, William Keck, Ron Krueck, George Schipporeit, Gene Summers, John Thorpe, and John Vinci; designer Jody Kingery; developer John Buck; historians Carol Callahan, Susan Dart, Wim De Wit, Paul Myers, Tim Samuelson, and John Zukowski. Each one was extremely generous with his or her knowledge, for which we will always be grateful.

We are fortunate to have many institutions in and around Chicago dedicated to the history of architecture. The Ryerson and Burnham libraries at the Art Institute of Chicago were valuable resources for books, manuscripts, and archives; Mary Woolever, architecture reference librarian, deserves our special thanks. The Department of Prints and Photographs at the Chicago Historical Society has an enormous collection of images of Chicago and Midwest history; we have drawn from it and are grateful for their cooperation, especially that of Eileen Flanagan. The assistance of the Chicago Architecture Foundation and Executive Director John Engman was invaluable in our research, particularly that focused on Glessner House, one of the foundation's museums. The Marktown Preservation Society, an organization in East Chicago, Indiana, dedicated to the history of Howard Van Doren Shaw and his architecture, was also helpful in our research.

Special thanks go to Jack Hedrich and Michael Houlahan of Hedrich-Blessing architectural photographers. Jack Hedrich truly made this book possible when he opened his archive to us. Whatever is splendid about the result is owed very much to them—the depth of their archives and their generosity in making it available to us.

We are extremely grateful to the staff of Harry N. Abrams, Inc., which shepherded this project from its very first stages and saw it through to completion. Our editor, Joan Fisher, demonstrated marvelous qualities of understanding, persuasion, and creativity in the two years that we worked together. To Leta Bostelman, Julia Moore, Judith Michael, and Paul Gottlieb goes immense credit for their parts in bringing this project to completion. Heartfelt thanks also go to Paula Rice Jackson, of *Interior Design* magazine, who assisted in the book's formative stages. We are also grateful to Ingrid McNeill and Marilyn Hasbrouck for their helpful comments.

Special recognition goes to Christen Smith, who provided research assistance, archival expertise, administrative skill, and many other qualities that were needed to complete what became an enormous undertaking. Through the entire project she demonstrated that sacred blend of patience and perseverance, without which many details would have been lost.

And to our wives, Kim Coventry and Susan Larson, we are deeply grateful for their support and understanding of this project. Better than others they witnessed the emotional investment in the book. We hope that no one appreciates it more than they do.

Chicago has been the creative center of American architecture for more than one hundred years, and it has too many world-renowned buildings for the role to be accidental. Chicago was home to the first skyscrapers as well as Frank Lloyd Wright; it adopted Mies van der Rohe and built Sears Tower. The city continues to attract the world's most ambitious architects, to visit, perchance to build. Its position in American architecture is secure.

It was not always so, however. Fate played a critical role in this story that begins with a sparsely settled town on Lake Michigan, named after the Indian word for a wild onion, *checagou*. It was a marshy place, even unpromising, but change came swiftly after 1829, when the Illinois legislature voted to build a canal there to connect the Great Lakes and the Mississippi River.

Well before construction began, anticipation of the canal caused Chicago's first land and population boom. Records show that one small lot sold for $100 in 1832 and for $15,000 three years later. The bubble soon burst, but the waterway and the railroads that followed nourished explosive growth that was unprecedented in any city anywhere. Meat packers and farm-equipment manufacturers made Chicago an industrial center. Builders and merchants arrived, and so did architects and assorted miscreants.

We can only imagine what Chicago was like before the Great Fire of 1871. There were pockets of wealth, but many streets were quagmires lined with hovels. Chicago could impress its visitors, and it could disgust them as well. So mixed was this image that when the fire cut its wide swath through the city, leaving some ninety thousand people homeless, many viewed it as a blessing—like a cleansing apocalypse. In books published after the disaster, writers sought to describe the fire as a physical force of almost unbelievable power. The image that stuck was hellfire and brimstone. Those who survived would rebuild something glorious.

Enthusiasm in the fire's wake was in no way illusory. Within days new buildings were going up. Within a month five thousand cottages were constructed, and many more substantial buildings were on their way. Quickly, land values caught up to prefire levels and surpassed them. Even the rubble that workers hauled away was put to good use as landfill to extend buildable land out into the lake. Three weeks after the fire, *Harper's Weekly* wrote that Chicago "will be made a better city than it ever could have become but for this fire." One result would be a "better building system."

This slant on the news did not pass unnoticed by Eastern architects, and many moved to Chicago with all due haste. Most of the newcomers, of course, had neither the disposition nor the skill to provide Chicago with a building system even remotely better. New buildings, like the old ones, were mostly dark and clumsily ornamented. Streets remained clogged. The most stirring innovation, some people believed, was the addition of salt in mortar; now bricklayers could work in winter as well.

Nevertheless, a few new arrivals did have a vision, and their names are etched in America's architectural history: John Wellborn Root, Louis Henry Sullivan, and William Holabird among them. Chicago gave these men what architects say they covet most: a clean slate for new ideas. Their designs called for bigger, more spacious, and frankly more beautiful buildings. As their ideas were realized, they attracted, in turn, other architects with ideas of their own. So began a succession that continued through the twentieth century. This was Chicago's architectural tradition.

It was Chicago's good fortune that rebuilding after the fire began at the onset of many other changes in America. As a rural nation became urban, the old world turned modern. Railroads, steel mills, business empires, and sprawling suburbs were new and powerful social forces. Each helped to accelerate Chicago's growth at a pace beyond anything previously imaginable. Each force would influence architecture deeply. Within two decades, steel frames, tall buildings, urban planning, and "modern" houses became part of Chicago's new architectural language. The city that had already opened the door to the West was now ushering in the new century.

EVOLUTION OF MODERN BUILDING

Modern architecture matured with amazing speed in Chicago. An early milestone came in 1885, when ex–Civil War officer and engineer William Le Baron Jenney completed the Home Insurance Building at LaSalle and Adams streets. This building, now demolished, was one of the first to use steel-frame construction, and it has been called the precursor of the modern skyscraper. Other milestones followed as the so-called Chicago School refined steel-frame construction. A few years later it fell to Louis Sullivan, a former draftsman in Jenney's office, to bring tall buildings to their next step, which was beauty. Sullivan designed them with such distinct elegance that architects from around the world made Chicago the most important stop on their American tours.

Other developments came with surprising haste, due in large measure to the ability of one generation to transmit its genius to the next. Frank Lloyd Wright, a former Sullivan protégé, developed suburban houses that transformed the idea of the single-family home. Later came Ludwig Mies van der Rohe, whose teachings deeply influenced the office of Skidmore, Owings and Merrill. Still later, SOM's Myron Goldsmith and Fazlur Khan were among the teachers at Illinois Institute of Technology to influence another generation, many of whom are active today.

This tradition has had a remarkably long life, but like any living bloodline, it has changed over time, even suffered its share of setbacks. The Chicago School seemed undone, for example, when beaux-arts architects from the East came to Chicago to design the Columbian Exposition in a wildly neoclassical style. In time, however, the fashion for ancient Greek passed, and the old Chicago language returned, imparting strength and simplicity to a succession of later buildings — including the skyscrapers of the sixties and seventies and even some postmodern buildings of the present.

Examining Chicago architecture as a language, or a set of values, is nothing less than cultural anthropology. It demands a broad overview, mindful that in the Babel of a great city, in the tensions of an explosive century, there came order. Economic necessities led to building problems to be solved. Solutions became fodder for

Opposite: Chicago Stock Exchange, LaSalle and Washington streets. Completed 1894, demolished 1972; Adler and Sullivan

Adler and Sullivan proved that office buildings could be large and utilitarian and maintain palatial dignity as well. One of the best examples was the Chicago Stock Exchange. Its ornate Trading Room was salvaged and reconstructed in the Art Institute of Chicago in 1977.

discussion and improvement. While good architecture never happens in a vacuum, Chicago was particularly fertile, buzzing with ambition, activity, and growth, yet somehow small enough and young enough for new ideas to grow swiftly.

The architectural tradition of Chicago began early and ran deep. At first it was strictly utilitarian, pushed by the need for economical and rapid construction. "Sky-scrapers," as tall buildings came to be called, were motivated by expensive land and a business district hemmed in by water on three sides. An early task of architects, therefore, was to master iron and steel, which could frame a building in a matter of days and anchor it into marshy soil, no mean feat itself. Other ideas developed naturally. Jenney and his followers found that steel frames allowed larger windows, and they could fill their buildings with light as never before. They also noted that these frames had a certain natural grace, and the simple lines of a well-proportioned skyscraper could have a form as impressive as a Greek temple or a Gothic cathedral. The need to decorate buildings did not go away, but it changed to highlight, not hide, the natural lines of tall office towers. In Chicago, a ruggedly beautiful, classic style of skyscraper quickly evolved. Such a building should be "every inch a proud and soaring thing," Sullivan wrote, "rising in sheer exaltation that from bottom to top it is a unit without a single dissenting line."

THE SEVEN LAMPS

Inventing modern American architecture was exciting but not easy, and it took its toll on individuals who advanced the cause. Henry Hobson Richardson died in mid-career, just after building some of his most influential buildings in Chicago. John Root died young as well, and it was as if the sheer creative force of their work simply exhausted them. Sullivan's decline in his final years was particularly distressing, and it was clearly the result of his refusal to compromise. Time and again, the stories of Chicago's architects are dramatic and emotional. As figures they have become icons. Their lives have been woven into epic.

Yet modern architecture did not appear in Chicago without precedent. Nor did Chicago architects neglect the past entirely. Quite to the contrary, the most thoughtful architects were true students who seriously searched history for its timeless lessons. In their reading, many Chicago architects found that one rather old book was of particular help in shaping the terms of modern architecture. It was *The Seven Lamps of Architecture*, written in 1849 by traveler and art critic John Ruskin. The son of an English sherry merchant, Ruskin was educated at Oxford, where he became something of an aesthete. The turning point in his life came while he was on an architectural tour of France and Italy and witnessed buildings that had stood for centuries. The monuments were lovely, he wrote, and time had only improved their looks. They were masterpieces of craftsmanship with masonry so precise "that after six hundred years of sunshine and rain, a lancet could not be put between their joints." Good architecture was good forever, Ruskin reasoned, and well-designed structures ever fresh to the eye.

In *The Seven Lamps* Ruskin analyzes what he believed were the qualities of this or any valid architectural statement. They were his Lamps: Sacrifice, Truth, Power, Beauty, Life, Memory, and Obedience. Of Sacrifice Ruskin states that great architecture can and should be costly, not for self-aggrandizement but rather in the exaltation of public life. (Ruskin meant cathedrals, but Chicago architects understandably substituted office buildings.) Of Obedience he wrote that the rules of proportion are inviolate; those that govern a classical structure apply to a factory as well.

Ruskin's treatise was inspiring for architects in search of new styles, and his Lamp of

University Club of Chicago, 76 East Monroe Street. Completed 1905, Holabird and Roche
In Chicago's fast and furious heyday, the medieval past was often invoked as a time of nobility and
high moral purpose. On a more practical level, the verticality of Gothic architecture lent itself to
great interior spaces that iron and steel frames had only recently made easily attainable.

Life applied particularly. Ruskin explained how truly harmonious buildings cause
sensations to the eye, how the arches and mosaics of Saint Mark's in Venice compose
"as lovely a dream as ever filled human imagination." This brilliant effect, of course,
was not because of rules and formulas. It occurred because the architect created
something that became vibrant and alive. It is certain that practical Chicago architects
had little patience for Ruskin's laborious prose style and probably skipped over his
breakdown of many medieval facades into feet and inches. What did come through
was that in any building even the smallest details must be organically connected to the
overall sensation.

ORGANIC ARCHITECTURE

"Organic" is Ruskin's word, and it was quickly adopted by the Chicagoans. Few
concepts are as important to modern architecture. As it developed, organic came to
mean that the overall sensation of a building—its Life—was more than an outgrowth of
form. It was simultaneously related to its site, its materials, and the needs of the people
who occupied it. To Sullivan, who wrote tens of thousands of words on organic
architecture, buildings could enhance human life in simple and profound ways. Tall
office buildings, for example, could relieve earthbound congestion and make the spirit

Following pages, left: Charnley House, 1365 North Astor Street. Completed 1892, Adler and
Sullivan
Organic architecture was an outgrowth of the site, the spirit, and the use of a building. In Charnley
House, Sullivan created a distinctively American home by making a connection between Chicago's
business barons and the princes of Renaissance Italy. The atrium in Charnley House features lively
ornament. Added interest in Sullivan's architecture lies in the way spaces flow and light floods in.

Right: Unity Temple, Lake Street and Kenilworth Avenue, Oak Park. Completed 1909, Frank
Lloyd Wright
The concrete exterior of Unity Temple points to the influence of Secessionist architecture a decade
earlier. Its severity suggests that whatever genius this building represents resides inside. "Why not
build a temple to man?" asked Wright. Inside, the composition of space and light are indeed a
monument to his trascendant skill at imagining and building interior space.

soar at the same time. Structure, purpose, and beauty could become one, like a fine, sturdy tree, each branch and leaf with a precise, organic function.

Frank Lloyd Wright expanded the lessons of organic architecture, forging completely new relationships between buildings and the conditions of life all around. To Wright—who began his career with Sullivan and collaborated closely with him on Charnley House (1892)—organic architecture led him to exaggerated horizontality for flat Midwestern prairies; it meant oak trim in regions where oak trees were plentiful. Most of all, organic architecture meant that space should correspond to or elicit human feeling. Wright, more than any architect before or since, understood architecture not as an object but as an experience.

Later in the century, as the concept of space became the touchstone of modern design, Wright rose to become one of the century's most influential architects. He was not the first, of course, to emphasize the interior. Nor was he unique in his conception that buildings could be designed from the inside out. But Wright's striking contribution was that he designed environments that seemed to speak a new and amazingly articulate language. He found meaning in light, in materials, in colors, and most of all in the lives of the people who entered his rooms. A Wright interior responds to them all. "Not only is the new architecture sound philosophy, it is poetry," Wright wrote. "Like poetry, this sense of architecture is the sound of the within."

A STRUGGLE FOR SIMPLICITY

It would be futile to describe in a few words the architectural character of Chicago in the early 1880s. Among the city's best-known buildings was the home of Marshall Field on Prairie Avenue. This was Chicago's former Gold Coast, the home of its merchant-princes who spent lavishly for homes worthy of the neighborhood. The Field House was designed by Richard Morris Hunt of New York, an architect who was highly praised and highly paid for his graceful eclecticism. This commission is more restrained than Hunt's more famous mansions, which often resembled châteaux with turrets and towers. "Must you wait until you see a gentleman in a silk hat come out of it before you laugh?" Louis Sullivan once quipped about one of Hunt's designs.

A strange self-consciousness underlay architecture of this sort, a feeling that wealthy Chicagoans should protest the plain industrial character of their city. This self-consciousness was to influence Chicago culture for many years—a "second city" mentality is pervasive. Nevertheless, a reaction to faux-French architecture and other false copies also arose. People who found ornamental European out of place in Chicago called instead for buildings in keeping with the surroundings. In 1883 a lengthy and well-aimed *Chicago Tribune* article complained that a Swiss-style cottage built recently in the city would be more at home on a mountaintop. It had little business in Chicago, which was filled with similar examples of ill-advised architecture. The critic went on to encourage an indigenous building style appropriate to Chicago and not an imitation of something Greek, Gothic, or in a style that belonged in the Loire Valley. "So long as this subserviency to the crude wishes of wealthy persons is submitted to we shall never have anything worthy of the name of architecture; we shall simply remain exponents of crudeness, the rampant self-assertion of ambitious nouveaux riches." The problem was that a Chicago style did not yet exist.

In the building frenzy just after the fire, out-of-place buildings were going up all around. Gone but not forgotten nor mourned is the old Board of Trade Building (1885), a hideous place that was located where a newer and far more elegant Board of Trade, designed years later by Holabird and Root, stands today. The old one was designed by

Prairie Avenue, circa 1900
Historic eclecticism describes most of the houses on Prairie Avenue, circa 1900, where French
"châteauesque" styles were preferred. The emphasis of most architects at that time was on the
exterior and not on the spaces within.

William W. Boyington, who won the commission in a competition that included several
more talented architects, and it testified noisily to Chicago's fashion for historical
eclecticism. Photographs show that Renaissance, Gothic, Byzantine, and a number of
less discernible styles were jumbled together like a medieval horror. Some people may
take satisfaction to learn that not long after it was built, its footings began to fail,
whereupon its high, ugly tower was dismantled as a hazard to public safety.

Many criticized Boyington's Board of Trade, but perhaps the most memorable
comment came from Montgomery Schuyler, the nation's most influential architecture
critic of the time. Schuyler, an early admirer of the Chicago School, had no patience
for pompous architecture. "There are not many other structures in the United States, of
equal cost and pretension, which equally with this combine the dignity of a commercial
traveler with the bland repose of St. Vitus." Schuyler also complained about anarchists
seen demonstrating outside the building, which was Chicago's financial center. "It was
very ungrateful of them," he wrote, "for one could go far to find a more perfect
expression of anarchy in architecture."

To put Chicago into a larger context, it is helpful to know something about
Montgomery Schuyler. Not an architect but a journalist with a literary bent, Schuyler
dropped out of college and got his first job on the New York *World*. Like most learned
Americans at the time, he was dedicated to the writings of Ralph Waldo Emerson,
Henry David Thoreau, and Walt Whitman. As he wrote about art and culture, he often
concerned himself, as they did, with discovering a distinctly American voice. Schuyler's
interests extended to architecture, and he discerned that many monstrosities being
constructed at the time were the result of two overriding faults: one was pretension; the
other was Europe. Both were inappropriate in America, at least in large, uncut doses.
Schuyler believed that a truly American architecture could be developed, but it would
depend — he wrote in his sometimes convoluted Victorian prose — on a commitment to
a style that expressed America's simplicity and honest strength.

In 1874 Schuyler got a part-time job on a short-lived publication called the *New
York Sketch-Book of Architecture*, one of the first magazines in the country aimed at
architects and not builders (who often believed architects were unnecessary). While
working at the *Sketch-Book* Schuyler met Henry Hobson Richardson, who edited the
magazine for a while and who would go on to become one of the most important

Franklin MacVeagh House, Lake Shore Drive and Schiller Street. Completed 1887, demolished 1922; H. H. Richardson

Symmetricality had no real function in Richardson's design of MacVeagh House, which was built for a wholesale grocer at a cost of $81,000. Instead, the exterior followed an interior plan with rooms and halls arranged for maximum light and pleasure within. Large arches, typical of "Richardsonian Romanesque," created a large open space and wonderful light effects in the dining room of MacVeagh House.

architects of his generation. Richardson's idea that form should reflect structure had a profound effect on the writer. Later, when Schuyler wrote a widely read column in *Architectural Record*, he lavished the highest praise on many of Richardson's designs — distinguished by thick walls, pitched roofs, majestic profiles, and great stone arches inspired by the Romanesque. Partly through Schuyler's writing, the language of "Richardsonian Romanesque" was adopted by many other architects pressing toward a strong, simple American style. With Richardson's examples in mind, Schuyler believed it was possible to repair "the estrangement between architecture and building — between the poetry and the prose, so to speak, of the art of building, which can never be disjoined without injury to both."

When Schuyler made his first trip to Chicago to write an article that appeared in *Architectural Record* in 1891, he claimed that the buildings he found there were a "welcome surprise to the tourist from the East." His curiosity about Chicago was piqued, in all likelihood, because Richardson had worked in Chicago on buildings just prior to his death in 1886. What pleased Schuyler was that the lessons of the master seemed to have rubbed off on other architects. Despite clinkers like the Board of Trade, Schuyler witnessed buildings of dignified simplicity and power and declared that Chicago architecture was the architecture of the future. This, he said, was the indigenous art for which America was waiting.

Franklin MacVeagh House: Even in Chicago the fashion for French interiors is evident, as here in the MacVeagh ballroom. But the strength of Richardson's design is more in its structure than in decoration.

Marshall Field Wholesale Store, Adams and Franklin streets. Completed 1887, demolished 1930;
H. H. Richardson

An original blend of Renaissance palazzo and New England textile mill, the Wholesale Store was an
appropriate symbol for Field's great retail empire. Simple, massive, and noble, the Wholesale Store
defined a new American style for a generation of architects in Chicago and throughout the nation.

Schuyler was most excited about a Richardson building that has since assumed the dimensions of myth: Marshall Field's Wholesale Store, completed in 1887 and demolished in 1930. Filling an entire city block, the Wholesale Store had masonry walls and went seven stories high. For many years it was the most prepossessing and influential building in the city's central district, called the "Loop." Before construction began, Richardson was interviewed by a *Chicago Tribune* reporter who seems to have paraphrased the architect, writing that "beauty will be one of the objects aimed at in the plans, but it will be the beauty of material and symmetry rather than of mere superficial ornamentation." This statement was direct and concise, and the idea was hardly mysterious to up-to-date architects.

The Wholesale Store commission was propitious from the start not only because Richardson was an innovative architect but because Marshall Field, the store's owner, turned out to be a fitting client as well (despite his garish Prairie Avenue residence). In those days the company that bears his name had a retail store of refinement, as it does today, and also a much larger wholesale division. Wholesale actually represented Field's principal business at the time, and the store was a gathering place for professional buyers from throughout the West and even the whole country. Appropriately enough, the structure that Richardson built to house this empire changed the scale of downtown Chicago in a single stroke. The Loop, until this time, was bustling but was mostly a collection of narrow commercial buildings on small lots. For the Wholesale Store, Field assembled an entire block—bounded by Adams, Franklin, Quincy, and Wells streets—by purchasing fifty-one separate parcels. There were no ready models for a project like this one, which provided a challenge that appealed to Richardson. He came up with something of rare power.

Since the Wholesale Store no longer exists, we can judge the building only through photographs and contemporary accounts. Reports are that it was simply the most impressive thing ever created in Chicago. Sullivan, often an emotional writer, called it "a monument to trade, to the organized commercial spirit, to the power and progress of the age." As late as 1921, Austrian-born architect Rudolf Schindler visited Chicago and wrote that Richardson's buildings "appear like meteors from other planets" in the middle of otherwise ugly cities. This is testimony to the originality and impressiveness of the Wholesale Store, which was meant most of all to be utilitarian.

The Wholesale Store was original but not without antecedents. Symbolically, there is no question but that Richardson was expressing the merchant's power, and that he reached directly into history for a starting point. Both Richardson and Field visited Florence shortly before the Wholesale Store was designed. It is no coincidence that the massive dimensions of the Field store resemble those of Palazzo Pitti in Florence, Italy. The palace has a massive beauty that could easily inspire an architect bent on simple grandeur. The merchant-prince allusion was certainly an attractive one as well.

But Richardson was no copyist. While he admired old Tuscan forms, he had other things in mind to give the building life of its own. We know from photos in Richardson's collection that Roman aqueducts enchanted him, and distinct notes of that ancient form also show up in the Field building. To reinforce the simplicity of the place, Richardson folds in yet another influence, this one thoroughly un-European. The rear facade reveals rows of large arched windows like those common in the most American of all commercial structures, New England industrial mills. Their practical effect, of course, was that light must have streamed in. Artistically, it was part of a demonstration that the essence of varied designs from the past could be blended into something original and cohesive for the present. The Wholesale Store strongly foreshadowed modern architecture — practical, original, respectful of the past, but in no way tied to it.

GLESSNER HOUSE

Another Richardson building, the Glessner House on Prairie Avenue, was designed with equal mastery. This one came late in Richardson's career; it was completed in 1887, a year after the architect's premature death at the age of forty-seven. Today, surrounded by factories, the house's stone facade has a desolate look. Even in its day it must have looked forbidding, yet the austere beauty of Glessner House amazed architects when it went up and has impressed them ever since. Mies van der Rohe visited it shortly after he arrived in Chicago in 1939. Later it was threatened with destruction, and Philip Johnson began an effort to raise funds to buy it and restore it as a museum. When a number of working architects took on the restoration as a labor of love in 1970 and needed to see Richardson's plans — so the story goes — a set was found among the effects of Mies, who had died the year before.

The relationship between client and architect is helpful in understanding this catalytic design. The Glessners were New Englanders who had recently moved to Chicago, where John Jacob Glessner was making a fortune in the manufacturing of farm machinery. Though the family was in commerce, the Glessners were also of an intellectual bent. The writings of John Ruskin and William Morris impressed them greatly, and they regarded architecture, dwellings in particular, as an expression of moral condition. They hired Richardson, the nation's leading architect, to build something different from the pseudo-French châteaux that then lined Prairie Avenue.

The Glessners wanted no less than a work of art. When Richardson inquired about the family's preferred floor plan, Mrs. Glessner protested. "Oh, no, Mr. Richardson, that would be me planning the house. I want you to plan it." During their interview, Richardson noticed a photograph of the stable at Abington Abbey, a medieval English

---

Glessner House, 1800 South Prairie Avenue. Completed 1887, H. H. Richardson

Opposite, above: Glessner House departed in many ways from other homes on and around Prairie Avenue, Chicago's first Gold Coast. Richardson's objective was truth and clarity in building, and he achieved it with this simple granite structure. The asymmetrical floor plan takes full advantage of light from a south-facing courtyard. Flowing space, undisguised materials, and a personal expression of the owner were elements of Glessner House that mark the beginning of the modern movement in American architecture.

Opposite, below: Richardson's attention to the courtyard of Glessner House demonstrated that the focus of architecture was turning inward.

Below: The Glessner House floor plan stressed natural light and flowing space — not careful symmetry, as was the case with its more classically inclined neighbors.

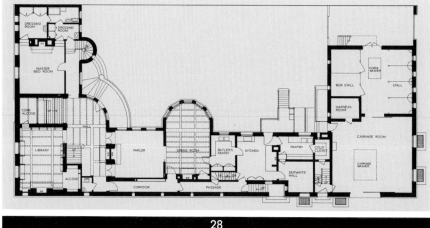

Above: The Glessner House dining room was refined and decorated with oriental rugs and fine furniture. Its most indispensable element, however, was natural light.

Below: The library—modeled after Richardson's own library—was the true centerpiece of this house. Glessner House has been one of the most influential interiors in Chicago architectural history.

Opposite: In the Glessners' day, a drawing room could be overfurnished and cluttered. But in the spirit of the arts and crafts movement, each piece was valued to the extent that it represented the hand of a craftsperson, anonymous or otherwise. Richardson was involved in the Glessners' choice of William Morris furnishings, terra-cotta tiles, and antiques to furnish this lavish home.

Overleaf: Dark-toned wood and oriental rugs give the entry hall and staircase a warm and natural light that was valued in all of Richardson's residential designs.

structure, on the wall of their home. Richardson asked if they liked the stable, a plain stone structure with a pitched roof. They said they did—it had a rustic simplicity much admired at the time—whereupon Richardson asked for the picture to take back to his studio. "I'll make that the keynote of your house," he told them.

This he did, but again, there is nothing derivative or pretentious about the result. The abbey gives Glessner House notes of domestic charm, but the facade also recalls the fortresslike formalism of an early palazzo. The fortress idea, too, was appropriate for its own reasons, since civil unrest was rife in Chicago at the time that Richardson was designing the house. This was highlighted by a startling coincidence that shows up in the Glessner family diaries. It was May 4, 1884, and the Glessners were sitting in their Washington Street home reviewing the final plans sent by Richardson's office. They were interrupted by an explosion and gunshots. The famous Haymarket Riot was taking place only a few blocks away, an event that helps us understand why the urban rich, even a liberal family, might look kindly toward living behind such a sturdy facade.

Richardson's reposed exterior is gentler than the average stockade, of course, but it is his interior that points to the new direction of modern architecture. Indeed, the very plainness of the outside walls seems to announce that the real interest of this house is inside. This would have impressed contemporary architects who were viewing architecture on a deeper human level and paying special attention to interiors. Social reformers as well as architects were reading Ruskin as the antidote to industrial society. The arts and crafts movement of William Morris, which started in England as an effort to reintroduce craftsmanship in design, gained momentum for the same reason.

Progressive families wanted advanced houses with good architecture inside and out. The most advanced feature of Glessner House, however, was something that might have been overlooked by people who focused mostly on details such as tilework and admirable medieval sconces. It was the floor plan, far from conventional but completely at one with the ideas of the period. Open and expansive, the reception hall, music room, and dining room flow naturally from one space to the next. This arrangement broke the unspoken rule favoring symmetry in many mansions of the period. It is asymmetrical, a choice that Richardson made for a very practical reason. Each room is oriented to an interior courtyard, and large windows fill these spaces with light. Light, as we shall see, became an obsessive concern for Chicagoans (perhaps because its climate so often makes it an indoor city). This was especially true for the Glessners, who spent only winters in Chicago, summering in New Hampshire.

Numerous features of Glessner House mark it as an early modern design, many of which were tied to the architect's, and the clients', emphasis on practicality, not showiness. One good example, atypical of the time, was that the central room of this house is not an ornate parlor to receive special guests but rather the library, a place used by the family every day. Creating a place for books where the two wings of the house joined expressed the added hope that intellect, not convention, might be the cornerstone of modern life. It was idealistic, but as an architectural decision it represented a definite turning point.

Because we think of Richardson as a Boston architect, it is natural to wonder why two of the most important projects of his career took place in Chicago. One answer that comes through is the clients. Field was certainly no typical client, nor were the Glessners, and the fact that such people thrived in Chicago had everything to do with the character of the city. Just as thoughtful architects found Chicago inspiring and promising, so did others with large ideas and open minds. Again and again, Chicago architecture exhibits this dynamic and its happy outcome. Architect and client interacted creatively and pushed against the limits of what had been done before.

Chicago drew not only architects but also writers, so it was apt that one of the most memorable American novels of the 1890s was set in a fictional skyscraper in the Loop. *The Cliff-Dwellers* by Henry Blake Fuller takes place in The Clifton, a prestigious Loop office building with safe elevators, central heating, and windows aglitter with the names of its fortunate tenants. Fuller made little attempt to disguise the social order that functioned in The Clifton: a beer hall is in the basement; better restaurants and a barber shop are perched in the tower high above.

The Clifton is a microcosm of upward mobility in Chicago, and predictably enough all is not well. Lives collide in such close quarters. Reputations are crushed. In an early scene, Ogden, a young transplant from Boston, is shocked to overhear the wealthy banker, Brainard, berate his newly engaged daughter as if he were "dealing with the concerns of an ordinary business acquaintance." Sadly, Ogden himself marries a shameless social climber and is forced to embezzle money to support her ways. The plot is full of cruel turns, but the central idea is clear. Lives are narrowed by ambition. The symbol is the skyscraper.

Few people read Fuller today, but he vividly portrays the intensity of Chicago life in these powerful times. He also shows the importance of architecture as a metaphor for power. Raw economic might was stock in trade for Chicago business barons in the eighties and nineties, and many used it to finance Chicago's fast-growing skyline. It was natural that skyscrapers should intrigue writers as backdrops to their stories. Some buildings were dark and leering, others bright and fantastic. In each case, buildings had the power to touch people's emotions.

In the real world, John Wellborn Root tapped a range of emotions in 1888 with his first great building, the Rookery, which is still the noblest edifice on LaSalle Street. Emotion was much on Louis Sullivan's mind as well when he designed the Auditorium Building with his partner, Dankmar Adler. The seventeen-story Auditorium was not only Chicago's tallest building when it was built in 1889, but it also contained the world's finest opera house. These are masterpieces of the Chicago School.

The Chicago School of architecture—the name was coined years later—counts Root and Sullivan as its most lyrical and successful members, but the movement began well before either of them. Its development actually goes back to the Great Chicago Fire of 1871 and remains one of America's central architectural stories. No sooner had the embers of the fire died out than rebuilding began. Architects migrated to Chicago in droves and shared the belief in a future that was nothing if not grand. Young designers had room to experiment with new building methods, and the best of them distinguished themselves with buildings of beauty and innovation. A few were artists who are remembered as the creators of masterpieces of American building.

WILLIAM LE BARON JENNEY

Now often regarded as the father of the Chicago School because of his work with

---

Opposite: The Rookery, 209 South LaSalle Street. Completed 1888, Burnham and Root
In John Root's Rookery, the "oriel" staircase that runs up the interior light well is an example of the building's practical plan but sculptural feel that prevails throughout the building.

steel-frame construction, William Le Baron Jenney began his career like many other architects who arrived in Chicago before the fire. The city attracted him not because it was refined, but because it was raw. Born in Massachusetts, Jenney went to Phillips Exeter Academy in New Hamsphire and then to engineering school in France. In Europe he learned the fundamentals of metal construction and presumably something about the artistic life as well. Indeed, Major Jenney (he served in the Civil War) was a bon vivant who would sometimes wander through his office with an armful of dressed duck for his evening's dinner and who would enjoy telling entertaining stories to his draftsmen. As a designer, however, he chose practicality over embellishment, so much so that Louis Sullivan, who worked for Jenney for a short period, wrote that the title of architect was applied to the major "only by courtesy of terms."

Jenney is most famous for his Home Insurance Building, built in 1884 and often regarded as the precursor to the world's skyscrapers. Jenney framed his ten-story building entirely in steel and covered it in "curtain wall"—one of the first ever to use the system that led to today's tallest buildings. Jenney's innovation was revolutionary, but it was not a huge technological leap. Indeed, there is plenty of credit to go around for the first skyscraper. Iron frames had been used for years in bridges and as interior support for masonry buildings. Safe elevators were another prerequisite for skyscrapers, and they made an early appearance in a New York department store at the corner of Broome Street and Broadway in 1857. Yet Jenney's complete dependence on frame construction, which some regarded as untrustworthy even after Home Insurance, was a major milestone in architecture. After it, there seemed no limit to how high buildings could climb.

If we resist lionizing Jenney as the inventor of the skyscraper, there is no doubt that he was an architect ideally suited to his place and time. His "bridge-frame construction" technique, as it was called, could cut months off construction time. Natural skittishness about fire also made steel frames attractive. Yet another advantage was that it permitted larger windows than were possible in masonry construction, which led to Jenney's development of the simple "Chicago window" (two double-hung windows on either side of a fixed glass panel). Jenney's lack of ornament very much suited developers, who grew unconcerned, even contemptuous, of matters related to "style."

Only incidentally did Jenney's buildings become classics. Lewis Mumford wrote that he "seems to have gone about his work absentmindedly—often instinctively doing the right thing but never conscious enough of it to give a rational account of his purpose." This is one way of explaining that Chicago architecture grew naturally from conditions of time and place, but it may be too condescending. Other critics have viewed Jenney as an artist way ahead of his time. Chicago's second Leiter Building, for example, was built to be a simple loft in 1889 but today is regarded as a ground-breaking modern work. Swiss architectural historian Siegfried Giedion got excited in his seminal work on modern architecture, *Space, Time and Architecture* (1941), about the simple propor-tions of the building that mirror the steel-frame underneath. He wrote that Jenney achieved what far more self-conscious modernists like Le Corbusier were attempting to do years later. "The Leiter Building marks a starting point for this kind of architectural purity and should not be ignored in the history of architecture."

Opposite: Home Insurance Building, LaSalle and Adams streets. Completed 1884, demolished 1931; William Le Baron Jenney
Iron supports, elevators, and larger urban buildings were all in their developmental stages when Jenney designed one of the world's first buildings to include all of these elements. Supported entirely by a steel skeleton and covered with nonbearing walls, Home Insurance has been called the "first modern skyscraper."

In 1872 the young Georgian John Wellborn Root arrived in Chicago with three hundred dollars in his pocket and a portfolio of experimental designs. Fortunately, he had practical experience as well—having spent a short time in New York as construction superintendent on the train shed at Grand Central Station—and landed a job in the Loop office of P. B. Wight, an early experimenter in steel-frame construction. Root was a confident young man and a discerning observer of architecture. As he toured the city, often with other architects, it was his habit to judge the buildings they passed as "architectural" or "not architectural." Those in which structure was apparent in the design tended to meet his approval; those that did not were often imitation French. Naturally, the buildings of his own employer were of the first category, as were those of Jenney. As he became more familiar with these buildings, they taught him a lesson—that real beauty in architecture was not superficial. "Styles grow by the careful study of all the conditions which lie about each architectural problem," he later wrote.

Root had an obvious talent for design himself, and just when Wight was ready to make him a partner, the young man was being pulled in a different direction. Daniel Burnham, another draftsman in Wight's office, was planning a firm of his own, and he believed a partnership with Root would be perfect, himself handling the business end and Root doing most of the design. So it was that Burnham and Root left Wight's office in July 1873, three months before the financial panic of 1873.

Business teetered between slow and nonexistent for at least a year, and then they got some residential commissions. Despite Burnham's talents of persuasion and Root's skill in design, several more years passed before they got the kind of work they wanted: tall

Opposite and below: The Rookery, 209 South LaSalle Street. Completed 1888, Burnham and Root

The Rookery was one of the first buildings in the nation to make use of a large light court in its center, which filled offices with natural light and enabled the creation of a glass-enclosed courtyard—an early retail mall. The building also became known for its ornament, including the gridwork of the atrium ceiling and ethereal designs in wrought iron and marble. Root's skillful use of space, light, and materials made this an influential piece of architecture when it was built and one of Chicago's favorite buildings today. The old city hall that preceded this building was called a "rookery," a place for pigeons and politicians. Root replaced it with something more akin to the aviary of our dreams.

office buildings in the Loop. When they did, however, they immediately distinguished themselves. Their ten-story Montauk Block, built on Monroe Street in 1882, may have been the first building ever to be referred to as a skyscraper. (The term was previously used for high-masted sailing vessels in New York harbor.) Burnham and Root, as the firm was called, built with simplicity and economy, the order of the day among clients. Root added a sense of proportion and art that pleased the eye.

Many of Root's buildings have been torn down. One that survives, the Rookery, is a masterpiece that shows how a commercial structure can be enchanting and practical at the same time. Today the Rookery has many of the same charms that made it successful when it was built one hundred years ago, and it proves that some advantages in an office building are forever—ample light for offices, for example, and an open area for congregating and shopping on levels close to the street. Root devised solutions to these problems that truly changed the course of American architecture.

Chief among the Rookery's features is a large central light well, which not only illuminates the interior but also permits a glass-enclosed courtyard. This became one of America's first retail arcades, an economic asset that also created effects that are far beyond practical. Balconies, stairways, and a network of beams and supports evoke weightless and limitless space—similar to the Piranesi engravings that Root collected. The Rookery was thoroughly modern at the time, making extensive use of structural iron, but it was beautiful and aesthetically resolved as well. It was the result of technology as well as the vision of a true artist.

Indeed, John Root was a most thoughtful and cultured man, and many believe that he, not Louis Sullivan, might have become the guiding light of the Chicago School had his career reached maturity. Root wrote lucid essays in magazines for architects about their responsibility to create an American style. Toward this objective, he saw Chicago as a great opportunity. Root was truly inspired by businessmen and developers whose need for tall, profitable buildings was so uncompromisingly clear. Root believed that by meeting the practical requirements of skyscrapers, he could penetrate the psychology or spirit of their builders as well. It was not an impossible objective. "Reason should lead the way," Root wrote, "and imagination take wings from a height to which reason has already climbed."

Root was the consummate *organic* architect, though the term was not widely used at the time. The Rookery's Richardsonian exterior, for example, was not an arbitrary choice. It was intended to stimulate feelings such as openness and strength, which are indeed what the visitor experiences upon walking inside. No artist was more orderly, yet none so elaborate at weaving architectural images in an ingenious way. Just how entirely Root's imagination "took wings" is evident in one of the Rookery's most important motifs. It was inspired by a bit of local humor.

This story relates to the building's name, a vestige from Chicago's old City Hall, which previously occupied this site and was known for two things: dirty pigeons and corrupt politicians. A passerby in an inspired moment named it a "Rookery." City Hall came down, but even as plans for the new building were under way, the name seemed stuck, which chagrined the developers, who preferred something more dignified. But it amused Root, and he immortalized the joke with laughing crows carved on the granite arch outside. Inside he took the ornithological image further. The atrium definitely resembles an aviary, albeit an elegant one. His etched marble panels and ornamental rails (later changed in a renovation by Frank Lloyd Wright) were winding and complex, some say nestlike. It was quite a rookery indeed—and proof that Root's imagination could soar at the slightest provocation.

The Rookery

In the Rookery, the delicate imagery of the place was cast in iron.

Frank Lloyd Wright modernized the Rookery in 1903, changing some of Root's details with new metalwork, marble, pedestal, and planter.

The Rookery

Opposite: The Rookery's triumph was its use of iron to create ornamental effects in a large open space.

Above: A recent restoration of the Rookery replaced these opaque panels in the atrium ceiling with translucent glass that floods the space with light, as Root had in mind when he designed it.

Below: Section of the Rookery showing the light court and oriel staircase.

The Rookery shows that the Chicago School was in no way bereft of ornament. A later Root skyscraper demonstrates how much elegance could be found in restraint. It is the Monadnock Block, built in 1891, where ornament inside and out is spare but wonderfully wrought. (Burnham and Root were architects for the first half of this building. The Chicago School firm of Holabird and Roche extended it a few years later, echoing much of Root's design.) On the surface, the Monadnock may be Root's plainest work, but it also may be his most thoughtful.

Correspondence between developers Owen Aldis and Peter Brooks indicates that they were strongly concerned with practicality for this building. It should have "no projecting surfaces or indentations," according to a letter from Brooks, who believed that "projections mean dirt" in the smoky Loop as well as "the lodgment of pigeons and sparrows." The developers sounded like they wanted a brick box. Predictably, Root satisfied that requirement and gave them substantially more. The Monadnock's elegance comes in part from sleek projecting bays that run vertically down the sides of otherwise flat brick walls. To us they are a masterpiece of profiling; to Brooks and Aldis they were quite perfect because they increased rentable floor space.

The clients were not entirely blind to art. It is through them that we know something about Root's innermost ideas for the design. Well before the developers saw anything like finished plans, Aldis wrote Brooks that Root's "head is now deep in Egyptian-like effects." There's no indication that Aldis comprehended why Root was studying ancient Egyptian masonry, yet there's a tone of admiration in his letter. Root, he said, was determined to produce a building "harmonious and massive and artistic."

The result of the Monadnock was a masonry skyscraper—Aldis and Brooks still distrusted steel—which impressed architects and critics around the country when it was built. At ground level, the base has slope and rustication not unlike a pyramid—a reasonable device given the weight of a sixteen-story building. From there it rises straight up, largely unornamented, and at the top its walls flare out ever so slightly. It is simple and handsome but so unlike other tall buildings that one naturally wonders what inspired it. The clue is in one of its few ornamental images: carvings of papyrus in panels high above the street. Combined with Root's study of "Egyptian-like effects," these reliefs lead us to the discovery that the building's profile is remarkably similar in proportion to sleek "papyrus columns" of ancient Egypt. Its projecting bays, moreover, have the graceful lines of the long, supple stalks of the same plant, which Root knew from his study of Egypt. It is not that the Monadnock resembles papyrus plants any more than an oak tree. Rather, the mere thought of Egypt provided the architect with a flurry of ideas to ignite his imagination.

Why Egypt? Here again the answer is involved but certainly plausible, and it begins with purely functional concerns. The marshy subsoil of Chicago, Root knew, was much like that of the Upper Nile. In previous buildings, in fact, he had borrowed the pyramid form for footings to help distribute the weight of his heavy skyscrapers. This may have led Root to the papyrus motif. And though papyrus did not grow naturally in Chicago,

---

Opposite: Monadnock Building, 53 West Jackson Boulevard. North section completed 1891, Burnham and Root; south section completed 1893, Holabird and Roche

John Root's all-masonry building was immediately praised when it was built—for its sleek profile, which delighted architects, and for its true economy, which impressed real-estate investors. Not only were Root's protruding bays an elegant new touch in the architecture of tall buildings, but they also added rentable floor space. (The Monadnock's addition, with an overhang at the roof line, was designed by Holabird and Roche to echo the original.) The building's wonderful proportions and restrained detail mark Root as one of the great artists of his time.

Monadnock Building

Top and opposite: Root designed with ornament *and* function in mind. In the stairways of the Monadnock Building, iron provided beauty and strength along with an openness that admitted ever-precious natural light.

Above: Section of Root's Monadnock Building with skylight.

papyruslike alliums did. One such allium, a wild onion Indians called *checagou*, had given the city its name.

What could be more "organic"? While this interpretation requires speculation, integrating functional elements with symbolic ones came naturally to Root. Images of ancient Egypt, home to history's most basic form of masonry construction, inspired his imagination to "take wings."

CLASSICISTS STRIKE BACK

The tragedy is that Root died in 1891 at age forty-one, just as he and Burnham were deeply involved in planning Chicago's World's Columbian Exposition. Burnham and Root had been made consulting architects for the event, which would open in 1893. It was a high honor, for this world's fair aspired to be the greatest in history. It meant they would be centrally involved in choosing the architects to design the grandest pavilions that anyone in Chicago had ever seen. There would be much competition for these commissions, and early on Burnham and Root declared that they would design none of the fair's major buildings themselves. This was a judicious decision and typical of Root's modest, equitable nature.

It was also typical that Root may have been overconfident that the Eastern architects who were eventually brought into the fair project would understand and adopt the architectural ideas that had evolved in Chicago. In fact, these leading New York architects—Richard Morris Hunt and McKim, Mead and White headed the list—were unreconstructed neoclassicists, and theirs were the ideas that eventually dominated the fair. Root, had he lived, might have influenced a more original American style, but he died of pneumonia just as plans were getting started.

Architecturally speaking, the world's fair was a beaux-arts extravaganza—and a clear disavowal of Chicago School values. The fair's main promenade, the Cour d'Honneur, was organized around a great axial basin and was rigidly classical in style. The buildings were intended as temporary and made of a kind of plaster, but they were whitewashed to emulate the most pristine marble. The effect of "White City," as it was called, was heightened to a fantastic degree by the introduction of electric lights. "Perhaps dyin' is goin' to be somethin' like crossin' the dividin' line that separates the Midway from White City," said a character in a popular novel entitled *Sweet Clover*, which came out shortly after the fair.

In her biography of Root, Harriet Monroe (the founder of *Poetry* magazine and Root's sister-in-law) acknowledges that the Columbian Exposition was a wonder and a success in many ways. Yet "John Root's conception of the Fair differed much from the White City of memory," she says. It might have been "a queen arrayed in robes not saintly, as for a bridal, but gorgeous, for a festival." Monroe admits that no one can judge an architectural scheme before it is completed, but she convinces us to consider what a Root-designed fair might have been like. There is some evidence. Before Root died, for example, *Inland Architect* magazine reported that he preferred a Romanesque scheme for the main pavilions, along with touches of colonial and other elements that could contribute to "a beginning, at least, of an American style." It is also reasonable to assume that Root would have had little patience for plaster made to look like marble. His early sketches called for festive colors. "You've got an exuberant

Opposite: Partners Daniel Burnham (left) and John Wellborn Root are in the library of their office in the Rookery. The photo was taken shortly before Root died of pneumonia in 1891.

Following pages: The World's Columbian Exposition of 1893 was a great popular success but "an appalling calamity" architecturally, according to Louis Sullivan.

Chicago Cultural Center (formerly Chicago Public Library), Michigan Avenue between Washington and Randolph streets. Completed 1897, Shepley, Rutan and Coolidge

Shepley, Rutan and Coolidge of Boston succeeded the office of H. H. Richardson. When they received the commission for Chicago's new library, their instructions were to build in the "classical order of architecture" and in keeping with the style of Chicago's recent Columbian Exposition. It was a disavowal of the simplicity and practicality valued by the architects of the Chicago School. Yet the library's massive vaults and ample natural light demonstrate that impressive interior space would continue to set Chicago's best buildings apart.

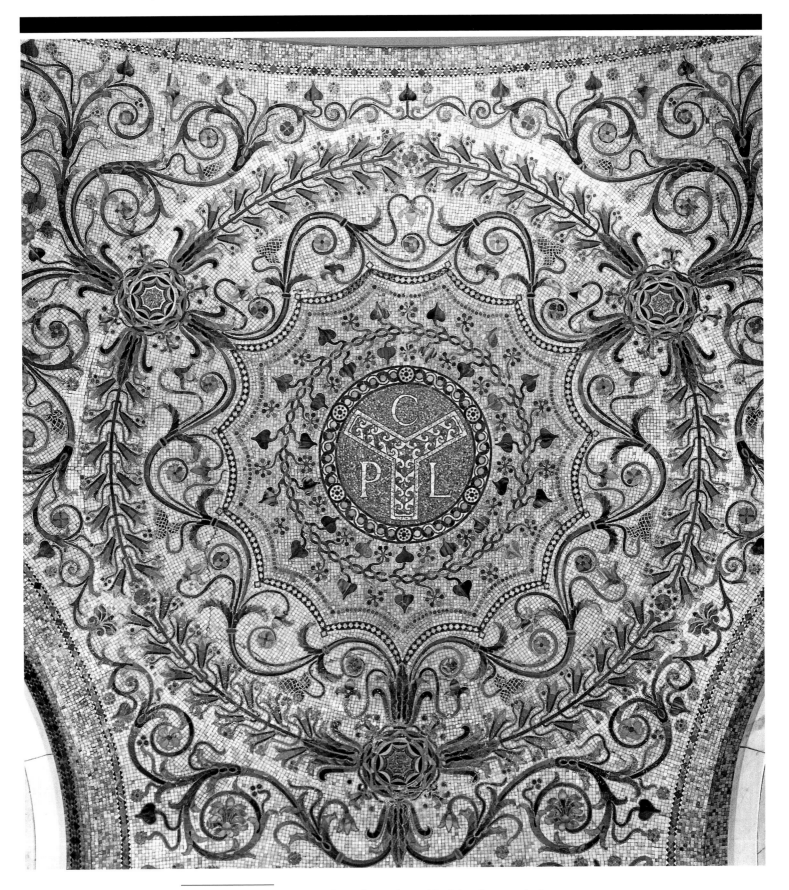

Most of the mosaics in Preston Bradley Hall were designed by Robert Spencer, who later distinguished himself as a Prairie School architect. The small glass tesserae were set at various angles to catch the light and enliven the lavishly colorful room.

Chicago Cultural Center

Above: Natural light, Carrara marble, and handcrafted metalwork make Preston Bradley Hall one of Chicago's best-loved spaces for lectures, music, and other civic events.

Opposite, above: The coffering was modeled after ancient classical forms, but the Cultural Center's metal chandeliers reflect a distinct fashion for arts and crafts, which was much in vogue when the library was built.

Opposite, below: The firm of Louis Comfort Tiffany is credited with having worked on the design of the massive skylight in Preston Bradley Hall, which was apparently completed by local craftsmen.

Opposite: Reliance Building, State and Washington streets. Completed 1895, D. H. Burnham and Company

The Reliance Building took the steel-frame Chicago skyscraper to its limit in terms of the size of its windows, which filled its offices with natural light. Clearly foreshadowing the modernist crystal towers of the twentieth century, the design was radical at the time but utterly practical. Even the white terra-cotta cladding was chosen for its ability to keep the exterior clean—a device that was only moderately successful.

Above: Orchestra Hall, 220 South Michigan Avenue. Completed 1904, D. H. Burnham and Company

When Burnham designed Orchestra Hall for Chicago's relatively new cultural community, he stated that its design would be drawn from the "Italian Renaissance, that noble and well-settled style, approved by the experience of centuries for external repose, dignity and effective decoration." What he did not say was that it would be achieved through the use of steel supports and other modern building technologies.

Opposite: Railway Exchange (now Santa Fe) Building, 224 South Michigan Avenue.
Completed 1904, D. H. Burnham and Company
Burnham's Railway Exchange was designed with the massive proportions of the Chicago School, but it still harked back to the "White City" classicism that prevailed in the wake of the 1893 world's fair. Burnham located his offices in this building when it was completed.
Above left: Despite its staunch classical looks, the light court of the Railway Exchange Building owed much to the success of the light court in the Rookery, designed by Burnham's late partner, John Wellborn Root.
Above right: Safe elevators were a basic mechanical necessity for skycrapers, but architects quickly used them as an opportunity for design, as in this cage elevator in Burnham's Railway Exchange.

Following page: Marshall Field and Company, Wabash Avenue and Washington Street.
Completed 1892–1907, D. H. Burnham and Company
Above: The four-story atrium of a section of Marshall Field's was surmounted by a Louis Comfort Tiffany-designed mosaic dome as impressive as anything a shopper might witness in Europe or New York.
Below: Burnham worked on the Field store in phases, finishing most interiors with dazzling *fin de siècle* style. Despite its pervasive classical ornament, the proportions and spacious interiors of the structure were designed according to the best lessons of the Chicago School.

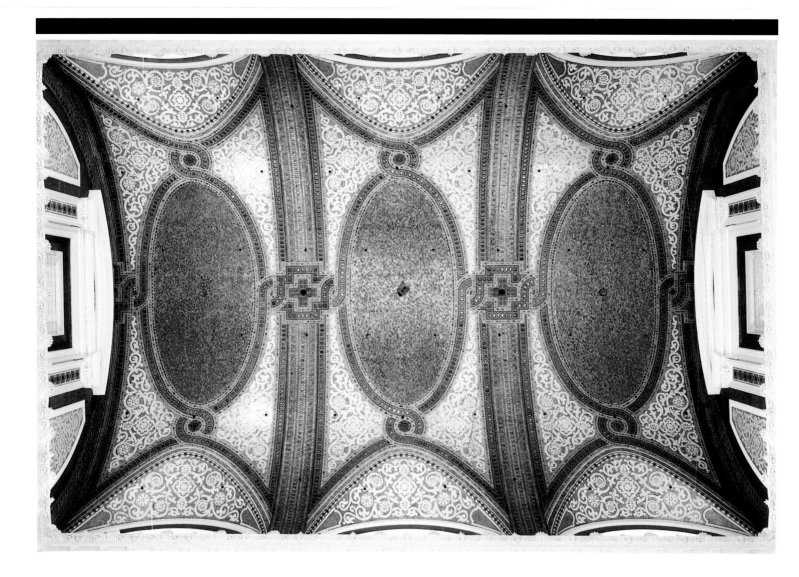

barbaric effect there—a kind of American Kremlin," said an English artist who saw Root's schemes. They had "lots of color and noise and life."

One wonders if Root really knew about the classicist forces ready to dominate this grandest of all projects. He probably would not have been totally surprised, as Burnham was foursquare in favor of the Cour d'Honneur and had even declared the Romanesque style quite dead. Perhaps it was the stress of artistic differences that contributed to Root's premature death. This is speculation, however, as is the fate of Chicago architecture if he had lived.

What did occur was that the lessons of the Chicago School lived on but under much different circumstances. Louis Sullivan, who designed the fair's Transportation Building—intentionally placed away from the main concourse—was clearly unsettled by the classical direction. "A naked exhibitionism of charlatanry," he called it, "enjoined with expert salesmanship of the materials of decay." More accepting was the editor of *Inland Architect* magazine who wrote that the fair gave historical eclecticism, which the Chicago School sought to shed, the "stamp of approval from high authority."

Happily, the Chicago School did not go entirely into abeyance. Daniel Burnham's practice continued to flourish after Root's death, and despite his predisposition for the classical he persistently incorporated the lessons of Root. Among tall buildings that his firm built in the Loop and other American cities, the Railway Exchange Building is typical. It is covered with classical detail, enough to satisfy the confirmed Francophile. But its graceful "big shoulders" are pure Chicago, and its spectacular atrium would have been impossible without Root's previous example in the Rookery.

FORM FOLLOWS FUNCTION

"First you have to forget what you've already learned," says Tim Samuelson, Chicago's leading expert on the architecture of Louis Sullivan. "The thing about Sullivan that throws people off," he explains, "is 'form follows function.'"

Form follows function. It is the maxim most often connected with Sullivan. Yet it implies that Sullivan's design is simple and utilitarian, and nothing could be further from the truth. Sullivan's designs—particularly his Auditorium Building—are filled with ornate decoration on moldings around arches, broad plaster friezes, mosaic floors, and carved wood paneling. How can the simple rule of form follows function explain an interior as hauntingly complex as the Auditorium?

The answer is not simple. Sullivan's beliefs about architecture ranged from complicated to inarticulable. One difficulty in the study of Sullivan is that he wrote impulsively and in such abstraction about architecture that only his devoted followers can completely comprehend. But a visit to the Auditorium's many incredible spaces reveals an architecture as intense and harmonious as the music that once filled its opera house.

Much of the Auditorium has faded; it now houses an urban university. In the once-

Following pages: The Auditorium, South Michigan Avenue and Congress Street. Completed 1889, Adler and Sullivan

When it was built, The Auditorium was the tallest building in Chicago and was regarded the world's finest opera house. Today it demonstrates that Louis Sullivan, who was thirty years old when he and his partner, Dankmar Adler, designed it, could masterfully blend rational structure with poetic ornament. In doing so he was instrumental in creating an "American" style when one did not previously exist.

The impressiveness of the Auditorium hotel lobby, shown here circa 1900, was in its proportions and in its marvelous detail—a virtual kaleidoscope of color, light, and form. The Auditorium—hotel, offices, and opera house—was one of the first mixed-use buildings of such size. In 1888 the Republicans used the building, not yet complete, to nominate Benjamin Harrison. One local party official declared publicly that it was the "biggest thing in the world."

The Auditorium

Through the combined skills of Adler (the engineer) and Sullivan (the designer), the Auditorium is a functional triumph as well as a visual one. The space had five thousand lights, one hundred fifty footlights, and other electrical illumination. International stars regarded its acoustics the best in the world. The modern stage had backdrops equipped for wavelike and rocking effects, and a rigging loft could hold eighty tons of apparatus. The theater seated four thousand.

splendid lobby, layers of paint cover moldings. A newsstand is anchored in one corner. While colors are now sadly drab, they were originally dynamic and alive. From the dark onyx at the base of the walls, colors once grew progressively lighter up to pastel ceilings. Samuelson describes capitals of columns covered with gold leaf "so bright you could tie your tie by it."

Some features we can only imagine, yet the lobby still provides emotional impact found in very few interiors. Huge columns appear to support a structure of tremendous mass. Leafy designs in plaster panels everywhere grow with apparent weightlessness from the walls. A broad staircase rises grandly through a monumental arch, then turns into light streaming in from the second floor. From the landing a visitor glances back at a mosaic floor of intriguing harmony. It is architecture that gives strength just to stand inside.

To say that Louis Sullivan designed pleasant spaces is like saying Henry David Thoreau wrote manuals for nature buffs. Sullivan, like Thoreau, was an intensely spiritual man and sought to touch something deep in the human condition. According to Samuelson, "Sullivan was very much influenced by the philosophical curve of the mid-nineteenth century," by transcendentalists Ralph Waldo Emerson as well as Thoreau. He was fascinated by Charles Darwin and responded directly to Walt Whitman's poetry. "Sullivan believed very much that man was a part of the overall system of nature. To him architecture was an opportunity to develop the relationship between nature and man's creative being." Thus Sullivan developed his idea of organic architecture, that buildings could be designed as an extension of nature.

The fact that structure could be artistically expressed was not new. Indeed, the lessons went back to ancient Greece and more recently to the early nineteenth-century French theorist Viollet-le-Duc, who explained that architectural beauty was the natural outcome of honest engineering. Sullivan admired the structural purity of William Le Baron Jenney. Perhaps most conspicuously, he was influenced by H. H. Richardson. Clearly, Sullivan had Richardson's powerful aqueducts in mind when he designed the exterior of the Auditorium, a monumental building that required monumental imagery to express it.

Sullivan was almost wildly idealistic and became convinced that organic architecture would lead to a truly original American art form. The Auditorium demonstrates how these ideas developed in his extraordinarily active mind. His thinking in this case went back to the original purpose of the commission, which was to build a virtual palace for opera and music, and combine it with a hotel and office complex that would generate revenue. The Auditorium was first a structural problem in the realm of Sullivan's engineer and partner, Dankmar Adler, who solved it with a unique plan and ingenious construction techniques. For Sullivan this was only the beginning. Because the building embodied a marriage between capitalism and culture, a new architectural expression was called for. Just as its multiuse function would combine commercialism and aesthetics, its appearance would represent a blend of reason and emotion. Architecture, Sullivan knew, could make abstraction a physical reality.

Sullivan's objective was achieved primarily in the interiors. The architect's genius, plainly put, was in his ability to blend structure, a *rational* expression, with ornament, which is *emotional*. In most aspects of life, reason and emotion remain separate or at odds. It is left to artists to weave them together, and the architectural triumph of the Auditorium is that structure and ornament — reason and emotion — grow "as if from the same seed," says Samuelson. The seed metaphor is especially useful for understanding the complex designs that decorate the walls and ceilings. "His principle is that the ground nurtures the seed, and it grows into a flower. The flower is wonderful to look at.

The Auditorium
With Sullivan, the power of interior space took on new meaning. Great arches and organic
ornament conspire to create effects that had no precedent, as seen in the dining room circa 1890.

It gives an emotional lift. But it is also an integral, self-contained organism. One part relates to the other. Sullivan believed that you could train your mind and do the same thing with architecture."

Stories abound about Sullivan's search for the tradesmen who could translate common materials into the art he intended. For the Auditorium he found a Norwegian plasterer named Kristian Schneider. Meetings between them would go on for hours so that Schneider would understand the feeling that Sullivan wanted. The architect was adamant that the complex botanical designs that he designed should appear to grow right from the plaster, not applied like pastiche. Compared to plaster ornament on clumsier buildings, those in the Auditorium appear as natural as ripples on a pond.

"LARGE IDEAS TENDING TO METAPHYSICS"

Sullivan's passions first took form in school, where he was a rebellious student. Born in Boston in 1856, he enrolled in the architecture program at Massachusetts Institute of Technology in 1872. There he took classes from Professor William R. Ware, known for his exhortation that American architecture had deteriorated into a gaggle of European styles, resulting in "architectural anarchy in which bad taste and unscrupulous practices abounded." Sullivan agreed heartily, but he still dropped out because the remedy at MIT was the endless memorization of classical Greek and Roman forms. More promising, Sullivan thought, would be practical experience. He went to Philadelphia, where he worked for Frank Furness, the well-known architect of uninhibited structures that in some cases looked like Byzantine fantasies.

He traveled to Chicago in 1873. Sullivan was fascinated by the activity of a city so recently devastated. It was crude and dirty, almost beyond belief for the Easterner. "But in spite of the panic," Sullivan wrote in his autobiography, "there was stir; an energy that made him tingle to be in the game." (Sullivan wrote in the third person.) In Chicago he applied for a job as a draftsman with William Jenney because he was impressed by the straightforwardness of Jenney's designs. He was accepted, and while there he took pains to perfect his tracing and drawing skills.

Sullivan quickly concluded that he ought to continue his formal education, so in mid-1874 he left Chicago and enrolled in the leading architectural school in Europe, the Ecole des Beaux-Arts of Paris. The school taught that the power of design was in the floor plan, and that exterior form should grow from a building's interior scheme. For a young man who believed that architecture had become a senseless conglomeration, this was an attractive principle, and Sullivan took it to heart. Again he failed to finish the course. The relentless classicism of the Ecole once again made him impatient.

So he quit and went to Italy, where he toured the great monuments. Sullivan was captivated by the Sistine Chapel, about which he wrote that Michelangelo was "the first man with a great voice. The first whose speech was elemental." Whatever these words mean, it was apparent that Sullivan preferred learning on his own than in the classroom. His educational experience is summed up neatly by biographer Robert

Opposite: Carson Pirie Scott & Company, State and Madison streets. Completed 1904, Louis B. Sullivan

From the quotable Sullivan: "I should say that it would be greatly for our aesthetic good if we should refrain entirely from the use of ornament for a period of years, in order that our thought might concentrate upon the production of buildings well formed and comely in the nude." The architect exempted himself from this edict.

Carson Pirie Scott & Company

Opposite: A powerful Chicago School loft rises from behind a delicate veil of cast-iron detail at street level. The store, called Schlesinger and Mayer when Sullivan executed the commission, is regarded as one of the architect's great masterpieces because of the clarity of its form and the richness of its ornament.

Above: Sullivan's rotunda was the perfect transitional space, defining what was then the busiest corner of Chicago's Loop and creating a small but evocative interior space. Restoration architect John Vinci calls the entryway a "cloister" that lies midway between the rudeness of the street and the refinements of the polite emporium.

Twombley: "Louis' architectural education had turned out to be a backwards tracing of academic ideological development. MIT had been a pale carbon copy of the Ecole, so Louis went to the original. But in Paris, he discovered the Ecole to be a modern outpost of ancient and Renaissance design. So Louis went to Italy. After that, there was no place else to go."

Sullivan returned to Chicago, where he resolved he could produce architecture that would be less historical and more "elemental," or we might say inspirational. He began to work with a variety of architectural firms, mostly as a freelance designer of decoration and ornament. Many designs he executed during this early period were successful, such as a large commission to stencil the interior of the Sinai Temple in the late 1870s. For this design in particular he earned valuable recognition, even if the reporters who wrote about it were baffled by how to describe it.

Sullivan joined Dankmar Adler in 1883 as partner in charge of design and decoration. The firm of Adler and Sullivan thrived for fourteen years, in no small part because of Adler's skill as an engineer, initially of theaters and the buildings that housed them. In these spaces Sullivan concentrated on his colorful and curious ornamentation. While most architectural historians are careful to give Adler due credit for the firm's success, Sullivan's contributions even then drew the most public attention. He went far beyond what was conventional. Again he baffled people who tried to make out just what he was up to. "Mr. Sullivan is a pleasant gentleman, but somewhat troubled with large ideas tending to metaphysics," wrote one journalist. Indeed,

Sullivan was almost apologetic when asked to explain the style: "That is an exceedingly difficult question to answer. I cannot give it words. I prefer that you speak of it as the successful solution of a problem. The vaguer you are in such matters, the better I shall be pleased."

It was, and is, hard to give words to Sullivan, though his message sometimes pokes through in articles that he wrote. Sullivan believed that ornament was as essential to some buildings as windows and a roof. "I believe, as I have said, that an excellent and beautiful building may be designed that shall bear no ornament whatever; but I believe just as firmly that a decorated structure, harmoniously conceived, well considered, cannot be stripped of its system of ornament without destroying its individuality." If this sounds glib, walk into the great theater space of the Auditorium. It is simple and majestic, befitting so large and formidable a space. It is refined with endless and subtle detail. Its vaulted ceiling crescendos from front to back. Also amazing about this space is something that cannot be seen: the acoustics. They are near perfect due to a complex relationship between the overall dimensions of the space and arched vaults above. When opera singers came from Europe, they were enchanted by the fidelity of the sound. When Chicago's Civic Opera moved from this theater forty years later, architects of the new Opera House used the old Auditorium as its acoustic model. It must be stressed that Adler, the engineer, deserves most of the credit for the way sound moves through the huge (four-thousand-seat) space. But the total result is the ultimate in organic architecture. Sullivan had often referred to musical art as architecture's nearest relative. Here they become one.

"TALL BUILDINGS ARTISTICALLY CONSIDERED"

After the Auditorium, Adler and Sullivan went in the direction of all Chicago—office skyscrapers—and for a while the firm was favored by many developers who wanted castles in the sky. They also became honored throughout their profession. In one of Sullivan's more lucid essays, "The Tall Building Artistically Considered," published in *Lippincott's Magazine* in 1896, he describes the art form clearly. "It is lofty," he wrote, "the force and power of altitude must be in it, the glory and pride of exaltation must be in it." He listed the three elements of a skyscraper almost in classical terms. It has a base, which attracts the eye; it has office tiers, uniform in all ways; it has an attic "to show," he wrote, "that the series of office tiers had definitely come to an end."

Sullivan was a leader, albeit an eccentric one. While the Chicago School developed with many local firms building the most straightforward lofts and office blocks, Sullivan could go off on marvelous flights of fancy. Yet his ornaments never hid the structure of his skyscrapers. They highlighted it with leafy, light spandrels and cornices seeming to float amidst the powerful thrust of the steel frames within. It was difficult to categorize or even explain why the buildings appeared as indomitable visions against the sky. In the "Tall Building" essay, he compares the skyscraper to a branching oak or a drifting cloud. In this context he utters the famous maxim of organic architecture: "Form ever follows function." When people saw his buildings, they understood.

Sullivan's career took its dips. He began to have trouble making the clients understand, yet he continued to elaborate on the idea. Witness the Carson Pirie Scott building in Chicago. It is a tall building, celebrating vertical thrust as skyscrapers do but also expressing the horizontality of the street. The balance of these two simultaneous effects is perhaps the building's most startling effect to architects who know how difficult it is to achieve.

Carson Pirie Scott is more than attractive. It is a textbook case of form intertwined with function. At the outset of this commission, Sullivan paid particular attention to the site, where the large department store was already a going concern. He watched its daily activity. What he discerned was a kind of theater—windows with merchandise and an audience of well-dressed women. With this function in mind, Sullivan devised Carson's most distinctive form, the cast-iron ornament that wraps around the entire base of the building. Like a veil, it provides delicate counterpoint to otherwise masculine "Chicago" architecture. It frames large windows on the sidewalk and makes walking down this stretch of sidewalk an event.

CHARNLEY HOUSE

Sullivan was the most influential architect of his time, but not because other architects could follow him easily. Imitation was nearly futile, so particular were Sullivan's solutions to the architectural problem at hand. On an abstract level, however, Sullivan's concept of organic architecture made a profound impression on the next generation of Chicago architects. Many regarded him as their master and hung on his many words. At the head of this class was Frank Lloyd Wright.

It is marvelously appropriate that one of the most wonderful interiors in all Chicago is a collaboration of Sullivan and Wright. It is Charnley House, built in 1892. On some levels Charnley House is a controversial work. One issue revolving around the work is its claim to be architecture's first modern house. Wright insisted that it was. Others say that is preposterous, that it was a rather direct borrowing from a small palace in eighteenth-century France. Another issue is its authorship. Who was the real designer, Sullivan or Wright?

Without imposing answers on these questions, what is clear is that some features of Charnley House are unmistakably modern. Its three-story skylight and spare ornamentation made it far different from other houses in Chicago at the time. Its unrelenting focus on the interior is notably modern as well. As for the Sullivan-Wright matter, there is general consensus today that Sullivan was responsible for the layout and Wright for much of the detailing. Long, narrow Roman bricks and plain moldings give Charnley House an overall horizontality, which we can attribute to Wright. The fine wooden screen along the stairway is pure Wright. The symmetrical plan and heavy exterior walls, on the other hand, come more from Sullivan. The use of so much wood in a house built for a lumber family was a note of organic architecture that could have come from either architect.

More important than the list of credits, however, is that Charnley House was a collaboration of major designers from successive generations. In it we see with rare power how architectural ideas can be transmitted. From an academic distance, specific authorship of one feature or another might be important. But up close, inside the house itself, the work of the older designer is inextricable from that of the younger. While Wright insisted that Charnley House was his own design, one wonders if the more enigmatic character of Sullivan might have enjoyed the difficulty that later generations would have in separating the respective work of two great architects. Charnley House shows that even in the most inspired moments, architecture is not created in a vacuum. Rather, it is the result of everyone involved—clients, tradesmen, and certainly collaborating designers. Architectural genius lies in putting together all component parts. Trying to break them up after they have been assembled in a completed design seems quite beside the point.

Charnley House, 1365 North Astor Street. Completed 1892, Adler and Sullivan

If the exterior was somewhat forbidding, it was because the real warmth and beauty of Charnley House lay inside. The house was built for a family with a lumber fortune, so the use of wood throughout the interior was practically and symbolically appropriate. The design was a collaboration between Sullivan and his young draftsman Frank Lloyd Wright. Successive arches harken to Sullivan's past work, and his design of ornament in the mantelpiece blends wonderfully with the natural markings in the stone. Amidst other Sullivanesque touches, the screen along the staircase showed Wright's advanced sensibility in a detail that would have seemed at home in many Prairie houses designed decades later.

Not everything that Frank Lloyd Wright wrote in his autobiography is objectively true, but the way he describes his early days working for Louis Sullivan has the ring of authenticity. Sullivan was a leading architect in Chicago in 1887, and Wright was a confident twenty year old. Their first meeting was simple enough. Sullivan needed a draftsman of medium talent to make finish drawings for the Auditorium Building. Wright wandered in with samples of his work, which did not show the kind of decorative work that Sullivan needed. So Sullivan told the young man to go back and try more drawings, this time with ornamental detail.

If it resembled a rebuff, Wright did not take it that way. "He looked at me kindly and saw me. I was sure of that much," Wright wrote in his autobiography several decades later. Wright stayed up late several nights to complete the exercise and returned to Sullivan with new drawings to get the job.

Sullivan looked at them and said, "So you are trying to turn gothic ornaments into my style just to please me, are you?"

"You see how easy it is to do," replied Wright, who knew instantly that he had said the wrong thing. "I had displeased him," he wrote. "Unconsciously, I had reduced his ornament to mere 'sentimentality.'"

Wright was hired, but the personal melodrama continued. He had to resign from another office to take the Sullivan job, and this threw him into a torrent of guilt. When he finally took his place in Adler and Sullivan's practice, he was immediately disconcerted by the moody Sullivan. Later, in the midst of haughty but less talented coworkers, Wright proved himself only after a ridiculous and bloody boxing match in the drafting room.

The situation improved, and the lessons that Wright learned in his five years with Sullivan became ingrained. But scenes at the outset of their relationship revealed an important dimension of both men: their emotion. Vividly, palpably, emotion comes through in the buildings of Sullivan and Wright, and it is what distinguishes all Chicago architecture at its best. While Wright could assume a taciturn outer shell, he was ruled throughout his life by inner drives that led him into erratic behavior. Yet these drives found brilliant expression in his work, and Wright went on to inspire generations of architects who followed.

THE HOME AND STUDIO

On a wide suburban street in Oak Park, Illinois, the dark shingle house attracts little attention at first glance amidst larger neighbors. Yet the house is a museum and a kind of shrine. It is the Frank Lloyd Wright Home and Studio. It is where Wright lived and worked for twenty years, and it is an excellent introduction to his architecture.

The house was built in 1889, the studio wing a few years later. While a guided tour of the Home and Studio illustrates the development of the Wrightian style over a period

Opposite: Frank Lloyd Wright Home and Studio, 951 Chicago Avenue, Oak Park. Completed 1889–1909, Frank Lloyd Wright
This was the Wright family home and Wright's place of work for two decades. It demonstrates a virtual catalogue of ideas from Wright's fertile architectural imagination, beginning with the early influence of Louis Sullivan to Wright's own unique mastery of light and space.

of years, it also provides sometimes revealing facts of the architect's life. One is that in 1909 Wright abandoned his house, leaving his wife and six children behind, and ran off with a client's wife. Guides at the museum do not dwell on this episode, but it is impossible not to wonder about it. It sounds self-centered and reckless in the extreme, and very likely it was.

This story clashes, tantalizingly so, with the mastery and control so evident in his architecture. Yet the Home and Studio, where Wright lived while he developed his classic Prairie style, was the scene of other difficult dramas of Wright's early life. These included continued difficulties with Sullivan, who was responsible for this house insofar as he provided the loan for it. All was well for a few years, but even before Wright bolted from his family, he had a violent break with Sullivan. The story is that Wright was designing houses on his own after hours, which was forbidden by the terms of his contract. So he was fired. Wright was fortunate and found clients of his own, but this house, with its occasional Sullivanesque ornament, recalls Wright's painful estrangement from the man he called Lieber Meister, his "dear master." It was not until Sullivan's woeful declining years that they were reconciled.

Today the Home and Studio has been restored to the way it looked in 1909, which required much research based on photos and interviews with the Wright children who lived there. It also meant destroying some changes that Wright himself made to the house years later, first for his abandoned family and later for a client who owned the house in the fifties. Yet the year 1909 is an apt focus for a museum of Frank Lloyd Wright, as it corresponds with the peak of Wright's Prairie style. Two decades of change and evolution had already occurred in this house, which seamlessly combines additions and new ideas in a relatively small structure. Nothing could be more instructive about the art of one of America's great native artists.

Viewed from the street, the Home and Studio appears traditional. The triangular peak in front may be more "modern" than other houses at the time—plainer and more

Frank Lloyd Wright Home and Studio

Above: The gallery in the children's playroom was a high and mysterious place. Its stepped-up railings force perspective and make the room appear longer than it really is.

Opposite: The stairway of Wright's home foreshadowed the pronounced geometry of modern architecture along with unabashed classical touches.

geometric—but in no way is it radical. Inside, too, many features appear almost antique. Plaster reliefs of classical heroes wrap the staircase in a frieze. Wright's mother liked classical sculpture, and he used it when he could, especially early in his career. The frieze is initially unremarkable in a nineteenth-century house, yet there is something slightly oversized about it. In fact, it enlarges the scale of the front hall—and reveals a direct lesson in Wright's subtle skill with proportion and space.

Another traditional touch in Wright's home is the partially enclosed inglenook, or alcove, around the fireplace. Finished in light-colored wood, it has a rusticity that we do not associate with modern architecture. There is an earnest epigram, "Truth is Life," carved above the fireplace. The inglenook harks back to old Scandinavia, yet it reveals something of Wright's future as well. John Thorpe, an Oak Park architect and a founder of the museum, explains that this inglenook foreshadowed Wright's command of interpenetrating space, the concept that two separate rooms could be made to seem like one, or vice versa. Here a roaring fire can warm the entire living room and become part of the larger space. Simultaneously, small benches built in on either side of the hearth create an intimate place where the family can separate itself from the larger living room.

These rooms seem conventional, with entry hall leading to living room leading to study—but the feeling is different. "It is like the walls are Japanese screens that have been slid back on tracks," notes Thorpe. Indeed, the feeling of space in this area belies the small size of the individual rooms, and it is helpful to think of the open floor plan of the traditional Japanese house. But again the touch is subtle, and to cite direct antecedents for Wright is always risky. In fact, Wright sometimes exaggerated his debt to things Japanese; he would occasionally appear in oriental garb so strange that it embarrassed his friends. Other times he resentfully denied that any such influence existed at all.

The originality of Wright's mind also shows up in the furniture he designed, which, like his structures, is often angular and geometric. Wright admitted that tables and chairs were difficult subjects for him, since formless old pieces could give comfort but ruin the effect of a design. There is no doubt that some of his early chairs are ridiculously uncomfortable, but he never gave up on furniture, and in the dining room of the Home and Studio we see how well he could succeed. Six high-backed chairs around the table form a "room within a room," a partially enclosed space around the oak table. In his autobiography, Wright wrote that dining is "always a great artistic opportunity." This was never more true than here, and even the provenance of these old chairs suggests that they had special power. Wright himself was fond enough of these pieces to move them to his home, Taliesin, in Spring Green, Wisconsin. Then after his death, his widow (and third wife) Olgivanna decided that they made her think of Oak Park, a subject not dear to her heart. She solved her problem by donating them to the Home and Studio.

Organic architecture is advanced in the Home and Studio in many ways. An example is upstairs in one of the most marvelous spaces in all of Wright's work: the

Frank Lloyd Wright Home and Studio
Opposite: Wright designed the dining set to be a room within a room. Floor tile, carved grill, leaded glass, and many other touches made this room a model for the American arts and crafts movement.
Following pages, left: The studied geometry of the Wright library focused attention inward toward the table at the room's center, where architectural plans were presented to clients.
Right: Wright's master bedroom: his celebration of Americanism is reflected in murals of idealized natives on the midwestern plains.

Frank Lloyd Wright Home and Studio
The reception hall of the Wright studio: an indoor-outdoor space to soothe even the most excitable client.

children's playroom, a great artistic setting for a child's imagination. The space is a great barrel vault, which appears larger than it actually is because detail throughout is scaled for children. Lofty but snug, the room has leaded-glass windows through which treetops are visible. High at the end of the room is a balcony, which the architect's son David Wright recalled as always a little dark and mysterious. The playroom was a place for curiosity and freedom, ideally suited to the spiritual life of a child.

Downstairs again, the interior zigzags to Wright's studio, where the children were not allowed and where the architect retreated from family life. The largest space of this area is the drafting room, which had a tightly fit balcony all around it with light pouring in over the rail. Its light naturally made it a favorite for Wright's drafting assistants. The room has the further advantage of drama, as it opens from low-ceilinged hallways that lead there.

Drama, of course, was Wright's specialty. In the reception hall of the Studio, with its door to the street, green and gold light streams in through colorful leaded glass. Leafy ornament and bas-reliefs of storks at rest are visible through the windows by the door. It was meant to be a transitional space, a calming moment for the excitable client, and it demonstrates how completely Wright could merge inside and out. "The outside may come inside," Wright wrote, "and the inside may and does go outside." It was one of his most important lessons and a vital component of what made Chicago the lifeblood of American architecture.

ROBIE HOUSE: THE CLASSIC PRAIRIE STYLE

The house type most commonly connected with Frank Lloyd Wright is the Prairie style, which was horizontal, wide eaved, and markedly open inside. In his long career, Wright's work ran in a broad range of styles, from his Queen Anne designs that he drew after hours while employed by Sullivan, to Taliesin West (his Arizona home), which biographer Brendan Gill describes unforgettably as "troglodytic" for its feel of a primitive cave dwelling. Yet Wright's Prairie homes are his most famous. They evoke a sense of classicism partly because their designs are so reposed, partly because they inspired many similar designs by others. After 1909, Wright went beyond the Prairie styles and delved into many other ideas of architecture. Still, the style remains the most vivid representation of Wright's mind at work, and no house does this quite so well as Robie House, which now houses the Alumni Association of the University of Chicago.

At Robie House, as in most other masterpieces of architecture, success was owed greatly to a client who appreciated and worked with the designer. Robie was no architect; he owned a bicycle factory and fancied himself an inventor. This house was conceived, the owner once explained, because he didn't want a cluttered Victorian home. Robie found such places to be effeminate. Friends told him that he ought to build "one of those damn . . . Wright houses." From Wright he got what he wanted, which included plenty of light. "Light has always been somewhat of a specialty of my disposition," Robie said. He also wanted a broad view of the outdoors but only with utter privacy from people passing on the street. These requirements were custom-made for Wright.

"Out of the ground and into the light," Wright would tell his apprentices at Taliesin, where he took on students beginning in the early 1930s. The phrase speaks to his use of natural materials — wood and brick — and his ability to connect living areas inside with the light, space, and flora of the site. Robie House achieves this through various techniques. The house begins with relentlessly horizontal lines, mammoth overhanging eaves, and long banks of glass, all of which tend to sever strict boundaries between inside and out. Wright talked about "breaking the box" that contained the majority of traditional homes at the time. Inside, this sense of interpenetrating space continues. The main floor, for example, is essentially a single room broken into subsidiary spaces that merge and overlap. The artistic power of the Robie House and its influence on other architects at the time are aptly described in Giedion's *Space, Time and Architecture*, which has become a sort of bible of modern architecture. Robie House reflects the "constant endeavor to find interrelationships between various separate elements." Almost single-handedly, Frank Lloyd Wright made space flexible; space was delineated not by walls but by light and glass and color. Robie House "brought life, movement and freedom to the whole rigid and benumbed body of modern architecture," declared Giedion.

Robie House is a triumph of physical geometry, and it is natural that Wright should control the small details as well as the large ones. Wright was not the first architect to understand the importance of furniture, accessories, and even hardware in the final architectural result, but he brought this lesson home loud and clear. Lampshades echoed the long eaves of the house itself. Leaded windows, which increased privacy inside, were designed with abstract patterns resembling the branches outside. Robie

Robie House, 5757 South Woodlawn Avenue, Completed 1909, Frank Lloyd Wright
Robie House is the classic Prairie-style home. Wide eaves, long brick walls, leaded glass, and a constant play of shadow and light were among its influential marks. It was built for Frederick Robie, an inventor and entrepreneur in the bicycle trade. Wright's design was conceived in part to satisfy Robie's demand for a clear view of the outdoors but without compromising the privacy and warmth of a comfortable interior. Wright designed Robie House inside and out with simple and recurring forms that interacted with one another in complex ways.

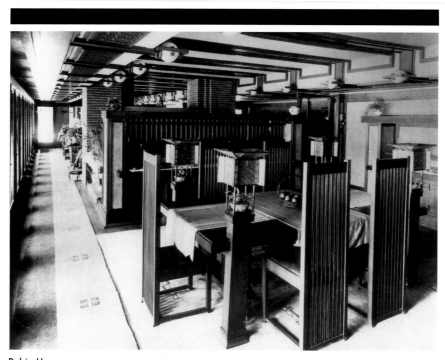

Robie House
Dinner was a moment of formality for Wright amidst spaces that otherwise flowed together seamlessly, as seen in this circa 1910 photograph.

loved the "constantly shifting patterns of color, figurations and the comfort of a very heavy rug."

Robie House today is much the way Wright intended. His dining table is now in the university museum, but many of the original furnishings have been recovered or reproduced. "It is very hard to remodel Wright's homes because they are so tightly designed," says William Hasbrouck, the restoration architect who has done much work on this and other Wright buildings. Hasbrouck insists that this is how the people who lived in them liked it. "I have met approximately fifty Wright clients," Hasbrouck says. "Each one has told me essentially the same thing. They say that their home is perfect. They say that they designed their houses themselves, and Wright merely helped with the drawings. And they all say that their house was Frank Lloyd Wright's favorite." If organic architecture means building to suit clients' most profound needs, Hasbrouck believes that Wright was the master.

The claim of magnificently happy clients does not square with the widespread conception that Wright constantly underestimated the cost of his commissions and otherwise abused the people who hired him. Brendan Gill's critical biography of Wright, *Many Masks*, quotes from many letters that illustrate the point. Clients were frequently stupefied by cost overruns and Wright's uncaring attitude about them. To be fair to Wright, the issue of his clients' money seems to have genuinely confounded the architect. Innovative architecture quite simply does not come from pattern books and is often costly for that reason. Illogically, perhaps, Wright insisted that the Prairie home, using common and locally available materials, should be economical. He no doubt told prospective clients just that, which caused conflict when it did not come true. Problems with overruns were aggravated by the fact that Wright rarely had clients of vast wealth. The nature of his architecture attracted practical types, as he admitted: "American men of business with unspoiled instincts and untainted ideals." These entrepreneurs often had limited budgets as well.

Against this backdrop it is interesting to examine a Prairie house that was unrestricted by cost, such as Coonley House, built in 1908 in suburban Riverside for Avery and Queene Coonley. The Coonleys were as progressive as they were wealthy, the types we now consider activists. They were involved in the Chicago settlement-house movement and other reform-minded causes. They were also committed Christian Scientists, which was a new and liberal approach to religion at the time.

Before their discussions with Wright, Mr. Coonley said he wanted "something colonial" for the land they owned in Riverside along curving wooded streets laid out years before by the firm of Frederick Law Olmsted and Calvert Vaux. Instead, Coonley was quickly convinced by his wife to hire Wright, and it was a good match. In their meetings, Mrs. Coonley expressed her belief that the new house should be a "countenance of principle," a phrase inspired by her study of Christian Science. Principle is one of Mary Baker Eddy's seven synonyms for God. It implies the oneness of all being and enforces harmony and grace.

Such thinking fit snugly into Wright's ideas about architecture. The outcome is a masterpiece, with harmonies that are dazzling and metaphors that are vivid. The interior plan is largely open, punctuated above with an unpredictable geometry of wood beams, skylights, and intricately carved grilles. It is a symphony of interpenetrating space, like a forest with streams of sunlight and overhangs of wood. There is unmistakable grandeur about Coonley House, but not because of lofty height as in a palace or cathedral. Rather its horizontality is imposing, inviting occupants to move freely, extravagantly about. Wright's idea for such a place shows up in a particularly flowery passage in his autobiography:

Coonley House, Riverside, Illinois. Completed 1908, Frank Lloyd Wright

This was one of the few Prairie-style homes Wright built that was unrestricted by budgetary constraints. There is an expansiveness and luxuriousness not found in most other houses by the architect. The gardens of Coonley House were designed by the dean of Prairie landscape architects, Jens Jensen.

A free country and democratic in the sense that our forefathers intended ours to be free, means *individual* freedom for each man on his own ground. And it means that for all, rich or poor alike, as the true basis of opportunity. Or else Democracy is only another Yankee expedient to enslave man to the machine and in a foolish way try to make him like it. Why not, now that the means comes to hand, let his line of action be *horizontally* extended: and give him the flat plane expanded parallel to the earth, gripping all social structure to the ground!

Though Wright's prose is convoluted, its meaning becomes clearer when illustrated by the wonderful spaces he left behind to prove his point.

THE PRAIRIE SCHOOL

In many ways Frank Lloyd Wright's architecture was the most influential of the twentieth century, but Wright was not the only modern architect of his time. The Prairie School was made up of architects who shared Wright's ideas and included many who earned fine reputations in their own rights. Working primarily in the Chicago area, they brought considerable attention to the work of "Western" architects, as they were otherwise called. While most Prairie School architects followed Wright loyally, the diversity of their ideas reflected the optimism and imagination that characterized their time.

These architects counted themselves as artists in quest of a distinctive American voice or style, freed from European traditions. Walt Whitman had been a champion of this cause, and his poetry became a touchstone for the Prairie School as it had been for Louis Sullivan. As Whitman proclaimed, American democracy was advancing, and the human spirit was being incalculably elevated by it. Architects were determined to keep up. Whitman had prophesied that a new man, an "American Adam," would rise from the western prairie. A direct inference was that a new architecture might be built on this very land. It sounded idealistic, but whatever else the Prairie architects believed, they designed houses with space, light, and room to move around freely.

Other social developments at the turn of the century made this a promising time for Chicago architects. One such development was suburbanization. The swelling of the outskirts of cities, especially Chicago, was promoted with messianic fervor by developers and social reformers alike. In the eyes of many, the self-sufficiency of a single-family home and closer contact with nature reflected quintessentially American values. So as rail transportation improved, suburbs around Chicago grew swiftly. Simultaneously, such popular magazines as *Ladies' Home Journal* and *House Beautiful* strongly advocated migration from unhealthy inner cities and frequently promoted the cause by publishing plans for homes that could be built economically on suburban lots.

The group of young architects who would become known as the Prairie School first came together in Chicago in 1893, when many, including Wright, moved into studios in a new Loop office building, Steinway Hall on Van Buren Street. Members of this group came and went, often sharing space, and they were anything but doctrinaire. What held them together was a search for something modern. As they discussed architecture—and they discussed it constantly—their rejection of tired architectural forms hardened. Their new ideas began to take hold.

Coonley House

Opposite, above: Coonley House has been called the "palazzo among Prairie houses," but its impressiveness is in its expansive horizontality and not in leering height that makes mere mortals seem small.

Opposite, below: Rooms become hallways, and this upstairs hallway becomes a room in the flowing, interconnected spaces of Coonley House.

Wright nostalgically called this group the "Eighteen," and it included Irving and Allen Pond, Richard Schmidt, Hugh Garden, Dwight Perkins, Myron Hunt, Walter Burley Griffin, and Howard Van Doren Shaw, among others. As artists they shared a number of qualities, the most important of which was a deep reverence for Louis Sullivan, about whose theories on the subject of organic architecture all were conversant. "A logical mind will beget a logical building" was among Sullivan's aphorisms that they regarded as gospel. Indeed, Sullivan and not Wright was regarded as the father of whatever movement the group believed it represented. Ultimately, a distinct Prairie style did emerge—much owing to Wright—but as the Eighteen started out, each applied new ideas in his own way, working hard to design simplified houses that needed most of all to be original.

To encourage this development, the architects formed a variety of different organizations. One was the Chicago Architectural Club, which mounted exhibitions of their own "protestant" work and held lectures. Subjects were wide ranging, and a frequent speaker was Joseph Twymann, an Englishman who managed a furniture showroom in Chicago. Twymann was a devoted follower of William Morris, the founder of the English arts and crafts movement. Twymann's message involved the role of craftsman-as-artist. He believed that the artist was first and foremost an artisan who was ever faithful to his materials. Thus the architect should avoid the temptation to make plaster look like marble or glass look like rare jewels. For followers of the arts and crafts movement, the mandate took on religious fervor and the tone of a crusade. The moral soundness of society depended upon it. On the surface it is difficult to see why Twymann's medieval-looking furniture and accessories appealed to the young moderns. What they loved, however, was that his fine woodwork, tapestries, and other objects had the imprimatur of a skilled hand, not an impersonal machine.

Many of these architects also became founding members of the Chicago Arts and Crafts Society, organized in 1897 and the second such group in the United States. Meeting at Hull-House, the group included social workers as well as artists, which was appropriate because of the conviction of Jane Addams (founder of the settlement house) that handcrafts promoted a sense of self-worth that industrialization had torn away. Architects, in fact, were warmly welcomed by social workers, some of whom believed that standardized home designs could do much to foster a sense of community. It was in general an intellectually active milieu, and the challenge of translating so many ideas into architecture was an exciting one for the Eighteen and other architects who joined them.

It is no surprise that one of the milestones of the modern movement in Chicago, and perhaps in the United States, came when Frank Lloyd Wright addressed the Chicago Arts and Crafts Society in March 1901. The speech, entitled "The Art and Craft of the Machine," quickly became famous. In it he praised William Morris for preaching simplicity in crafts and construction as a way to combat "the innate vulgarity of theocratic impulse in art as opposed to democratic." Yet Morris's disdain for machines, Wright insisted, was misdirected. Machines represented "the modern Sphinx—whose riddle the artist must solve." To illustrate he used the most obvious example for an architect interested in building homes—wood. "The machine teaches us," he said,

Opposite: Clock, 1912, designed by George Grant Elmslie for Henry B. Babson House, Riverside (Louis B. Sullivan)

Prairie School architect Elmslie was responsible for much ornamental detail in the buildings of Sullivan, his long-time master. Mahagony and brass inlay reflected his respect for traditional materials and for the people who worked with them. Smooth surfaces and straight lines brought the machine age to bear and prefigured the streamlined styles that would be fashionable in the twenties.

Pleasant Home, Home Avenue and Pleasant Street, Oak Park. Completed 1899,
George W. Maher

Pleasant Home remains one of Maher's best-known examples of his "rhythm motif" theory, conceived as a way to establish a truly American style. The horizontal lines of his architecture demonstrate his connection with the Prairie School (and Oak Parker Frank Lloyd Wright). His approach to ornament, however, was entirely original and was drawn from local images such as honeysuckle (symbolic of friendship). The lion's head ornamentation represents the Pleasant Home client, commercial banker John Farson. Photograph taken circa 1900.

Below: The upstairs hall (circa 1920) of Pleasant Home has Sullivanesque arches, interpenetrating space, and definite touches of the arts and crafts movement.

Opposite: Where other designers might have used classical forms, Maher's carvings, as here in the dining room, were entirely original, with an emphasis on the king of the jungle.

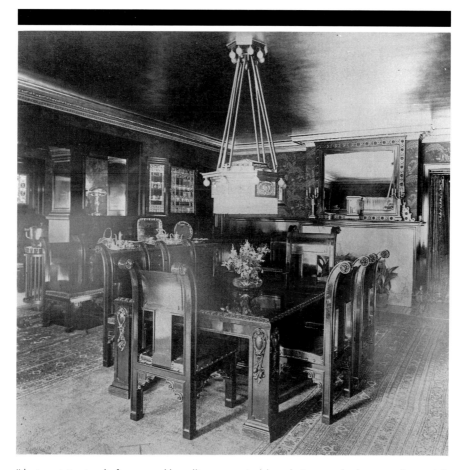

"that certain simple forms and handling are suitable to bring out the beauty of wood." The true beauty of wood was not in "fussy" carving, Wright said, but rather in its natural grain, which could be best brought out by mechanical tools to cut and smooth.

The concept of arts and crafts, variously applied, became a keynote of Prairie architects. Their interpretations ranged from houses reminiscent of medieval England to interiors influenced by the Austrian Secession, a group that combined notes of arts and crafts, art nouveau, and other styles. They became intensely interested in the truthful use of materials in every possible detail. "Art and Crafts stands for the idiomatic use of materials — leaded glass in a leaded glass way, wooden structures in the way called for by wood," architect Elmer Grey declared in *Architectural Record* in 1907. Grey, who would later become a partner of Myron Hunt, admitted that the bigness of modern construction and complexity of mechanical systems such as elevators and electric lights militated against craftsmanship in many aspects of building. Yet Grey called for a fellowship between architects and tradespeople and recommended that the trades assemble permanently in a central exhibit hall, where leaded-glass makers, metal-workers, tile painters, and brick manufacturers could show their wares in a place convenient for architects. Grey's idea was not immediately realized, but no one disagreed. Craftsmanship should be prominent throughout the modern house.

This seemed like a level-headed approach, but other architects who are identified with the Prairie School published notions that went into fuzzier realms. One of Chicago's most successful residential architects at the turn of the century, George Washington Maher, wrote in *Architectural Record* that truly modern design would evolve only when architects had the courage to set old forms entirely aside and develop truly personal styles. Maher's florid prose explained that architects must thoroughly penetrate the mind of the client, since architecture springs from deep inside the psyche.

Long ago, he wrote, Greeks expressed their distinctive sense of rational order in architecture, and the Goth, "cradled in mysticism, gave expression to his aspiration in the perpendicular line." Maher's logic followed that modern homes should be "influenced by local color and atmosphere in surrounding flora and nature. With their vital inspiration at hand, the design naturally crystalizes and motifs appear which being consistently utilized will make each object, construction, furnishing or decoration related."

Maher's "motif-rhythm theory," as he called his approach, encouraged the repetition of symbols from nature, such as the honeysuckle, which represented friendship. He also found inspiration in the personalities of his clients. In his design of Pleasant Home in Oak Park for investment banker John Farson, Maher fixed on the image of the lion's head, which he used as exterior ornament, on mantels, in carved furniture, and wherever conventional ornament might otherwise appear. The resulting house, built in 1897, was an expression of Farson's individuality. It was also an original, even strange, piece of architecture. Maher's designs prompted critics to suggest that "independence and courage can be misapplied," and wondered if the eccentric Maher was less focused on nature or his clients than he was on "expressing his own needs and temperament."

MADLENER HOUSE

Despite high-flown rhetoric, early Prairie houses were often successful when their objectives were understated. One of the most distinctive homes on Chicago's North Side is Madlener House, now home of the Graham Foundation for The Advanced Studies in the Fine Arts. Designed by Richard Schmidt with associate Hugh Garden for a wealthy brewing family, its exterior proportions resemble those of an Italian Renaissance palazzo but with distinct simplicity and absence of ornamentation. Madlener House was strikingly modern when it was built in 1902, and influences on it were varied. Mindful of the Chicago School—and the belief that buildings should express their true structure—Schmidt also appears to have been influenced by examples of Secessionist and German arts and crafts architecture then being published in German magazines. (Schmidt was German, having immigrated with his parents at a young age.) Modern Europeans were much concerned with structure. They experimented with radically simplified Greek and Roman forms and even endowed the factories they built with fine classical lines and proportions. So with one foot in the Chicago School and the other in Europe, Schmidt and Garden achieved a design that was "stately without being grandiose," as one critic described the exterior of Madlener House shortly after it was built.

Inside Madlener House, the architects went to the edge of being modern but no further. Large, interpenetrating spaces certainly are influenced by Prairie ideas. Its rich finishes are likewise up-to-date, with large panels of highly polished French walnut and intricate geometric detail in moldings, a note of the Austrian Secession. What is lacking, however, is an organic relationship between interior and exterior. The critic who found the exterior of Madlener House so comely, for example, objected when he

Opposite: Madlener House, 4 West Burton Place. Completed 1902, Richard E. Schmidt
Above: It has the presence of a Renaissance palazzo, but its simple lines and precise proportions can also be ascribed to the commercial buildings of the Chicago School, which held important lessons for such Prairie architects as Schmidt and his assistant, Hugh Garden.
Below: Complex original ornamentation was at home in the Chicago of Louis Sullivan, but Schmidt's design in the Madlener House doorway also owes much to the Secessionists.

Madlener House

Above: Love of material—a Prairie School keynote—is evident in the French walnut used throughout the interior of Madlener House.

Opposite: Within the rectilinear Madlener House, a touch of Art Nouveau is found above the hearth.

got inside. Windows that seemed well proportioned from the street were actually too small to bring maximum light to the space inside. Its furniture had little to do with the innovation of Prairie-style designers; it was only faintly modern, if at all.

One way of analyzing Schmidt and Garden is by understanding that they were in command of modern architecture without being truly modern themselves. They were eclectic designers, and the inference is that they were not driven by a deep conviction to advance the cause of modern architecture. This is borne out by a remark of Hugh Garden in which he said that his experience had demonstrated to him the ideal style for any type of structure: Tudor for country estates, Renaissance for city homes, Chicago School for commercial buildings. Such a remark must have sounded like blasphemy to the true proponent of the Prairie School. Perhaps Garden was simply more candid than other architects. Or he and Schmidt had a rare gift for making old formulas appear original. At any rate, Madlener House remains a successful and handsome building.

WALTER BURLEY GRIFFIN

In times that teem with new ideas, the artists who make lasting contributions are often those who focus on relatively narrow problems and make breakthroughs in solving them. One such Prairie School architect was Walter Burley Griffin, whose style, especially early in his career, was deeply influenced by Frank Lloyd Wright. This is not surprising, since he worked in Wright's Oak Park studio and had charge of the practice in Wright's absence. Griffin went out on his own in 1905 and made his mark outside the mainstream of most Prairie architects. Griffin's direction diverged in two principal ways. One is that he was intrigued with neighborhood and city planning; another is that he left America for Australia in mid-career.

The story of Griffin's career begins when he was a boy in Chicago watching the construction of the 1893 world's fair. Whatever else the White City would mean to architecture, the audacity of the Cour d'Honneur and the vast, winding greenbelts that surrounded it dazzled Griffin. The blend of architecture with landscape became Griffin's particular interest. In architecture school at the University of Illinois, he took a number of horticulture courses as electives. He was later exposed to the ideas of Jens Jensen, who was establishing a separate "Prairie" tradition in landscape architecture. Jensen designed public parks and private landscapes with an understanding of ecology that was uncommon for his time, highlighting natural landforms and concentrating on native midwestern plants. Such thinking had obvious appeal for architects with an "organic" turn of mind—Jensen collaborated with Wright on several homes, including the Coonley House.

When Griffin started his own practice, he embarked on several projects in which he worked out exterior space in much the way other architects designed interiors. Often they were small-scale works, such as the Comstock Houses, a pair of homes in Evanston. These detached, single-family structures shared a garden and a garage

Comstock Homes, Ashland Avenue and Church Street, Evanston. Completed 1912, Walter Burley Griffin

Above: In Comstock Homes, a pair of suburban houses designed for next-door neighbors, Griffin applied the lessons of his mentor, Frank Lloyd Wright, about flowing space and then took them a step further. In this case, the two structures share a yard and sunken garden with the effect that exterior spaces interpenetrate and overlap much as do the rooms inside. The home at 1416 Church Street is shown here.

Below: Griffin brought a true sculptural quality to his architecture. His designs, here a detail from Comstock Homes, often seemed to float in three dimensions.

between them, and just as the rooms of typical Prairie homes overlap and interpenetrate, so does exterior space around these homes. This was not previously common in suburbs, and Griffin went on to incorporate the idea of shared space in other neighborhoods that he was hired to lay out. Such planning projects were immediately praised by contemporary critics for their democratic spirit. "Always there is that consideration in his town planning problems of the convenience and happiness of all its citizens," *Western Architect* magazine wrote in an article about Griffin. Living in one of his houses "becomes not a thing of joy to him alone but an integral part of a symmetrical plan which adds to the beauty and value of his neighbors' belongings."

One can wonder what might have been Griffin's—and Chicago's—fate had he remained in the Midwest. In 1912 he entered and won first prize in an international competition to design Australia's new capital city of Canberra. Griffin's scheme included a scenic river, swelling lakes, and vistas of nearby mountains. It combined formal boulevards and naturalistic greenswards, recalling the 1893 Columbian Exposition as well as the Chicago Plan of Daniel Burnham. The opportunity to execute this design prompted Griffin to move to Australia to oversee Canberra's development and also design buildings that he hoped would suit the Australian character. Griffin's career was hurt, however, by the onset of World War I, which disrupted plans to build the new

Church of All Souls, 1407 Chicago Avenue, Evanston. Completed 1903, demolished 1960; Marion Mahony Griffin

Previous page: Marion Mahony Griffin was one of Wright's most talented protégées. She later married Walter Burley Griffin, and together they left America for Australia. Her first scheme for the church was low in height and domestic in scale but the Unitarians who were her clients preferred something Gothic. Still the finished design of random-cut limestone demonstrates an important lesson of the Prairie School—that the strongest architectural statements look like they have been there forever.

Above: The interior of the Church of All Souls featured dignified modesty wrought of broad stucco surfaces and wood trim.

Below: Floor plan of the Church of All Souls.

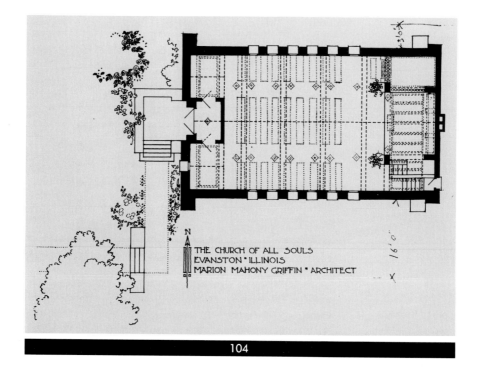

THE CHURCH OF ALL SOULS
EVANSTON · ILLINOIS
MARION MAHONY GRIFFIN · ARCHITECT

city. His fortunes were further damaged by the fact that ex-soldiers of the British Empire were in charge of Canberra. It is easy to imagine that Griffin's populist views and pacifist leanings did not help his cause with this coterie, and his hopes to oversee Canberra's development dissolved. Nevertheless, Griffin remained in Australia, working on private and a few public commissions. He and his wife, Marion Mahony, another former Wright protégée, also spent a period of time in India, where they designed a university library and a number of other buildings. Later in his career, which ended with his sudden death in 1937, Griffin devised a building system—concrete "knitblocks" that could be assembled into a variety of practical forms. This system was particularly suited for Australia, which suffered from a shortage of construction lumber.

THE PRAIRIE SCHOOL CLOSES

Other architects of the period demonstrate the various directions of the Prairie School. Among them, no one personified its idealism more than George Grant Elmslie. A draftsman and designer in the office of Louis Sullivan from 1889 to 1909, Elmslie became a skilled specialist in Sullivanesque ornament. Elmslie is notable not only because he was talented, but he was also unstintingly loyal. He was the last employee to remain with Sullivan as the practice sank. Even after Sullivan's death, Elmslie continued to exalt the humanism and poetry of the master's work.

Elmslie opened his own office in 1910 with another progressive Chicago architect, William Purcell, and for about ten years they enjoyed a busy practice. As members of an arts and crafts offshoot called the "bungalow movement," they built houses that combined the craftwork of the Prairie style with strict middle-class economy. Several of Purcell and Elmslie's houses in the Chicago area were influential, but the architects lacked the single-mindedness that fame seems to require. Unfortunately, their success never met their promise.

Purcell and Elmslie also designed a number of commercial structures, the most enchanting of which was the Edison Shop on Wabash Avenue. It was a four-story storefront with open balconies, and it seemed almost residential. If city streets everywhere were lined with buildings as open and friendly as this one seems to have been (only photographs remain), urban life may have turned out much more gentle indeed.

Purcell and Elmslie did not repeat this performance. Purcell went into semiretirement in 1920 because of ill health. Elmslie, like so many architects, ended his career on a disenchanted note. For one thing, World War I had drained idealism from society, and fewer clients were interested in his frankly progressive houses. Elmslie was reduced to designing banks and commercial buildings on behalf of other, often lesser, architects who got the credit for them.

A final irony of George Elmslie's career provides insight into the final stages of the Prairie School and its relationship to what followed. By the thirties, with the advent in America of modernists from Europe, some scholars noted that Purcell and Elmslie represented a historical link between the Prairie School and the International style of Mies van der Rohe and others. The assertion was that Purcell and Elmslie simplified the Wrightian style and further reduced it to its elemental geometry. When this connection was suggested to Elmslie late in his life, however, he rejected it immediately. He protested that the Europeans designed according to "formula" and not "inspiration." Nevertheless, the theory that the late Prairie School led logically to what succeeded it is at least arguable. Elmslie's rather bitter denial unfortunately shows how architecture moves on and often leaves its eloquent messengers behind.

The architects who dedicated themselves to modern and democratic ideas were not always favored by an important, and growing, class of client in Chicago—wealthy businessmen and their heirs who could afford the finest and most expensive homes possible. Families with large fortunes and aristocratic pretensions were often deaf to the aesthetic concerns implied by organic architecture. They were unfazed when Sullivan railed against architecture that simply copied designs from elsewhere. They paid little attention to the fact that the Prairie style, conceived in the Midwest, was being praised around the world as something of true artistic importance. Instead, clients with the greatest means usually ordered traditional houses, most often modeled after European estates from distant centuries.

The gulf that separates the group around Wright from the more traditional Chicago architects of the time, such as Howard Van Doren Shaw and David Adler, appears wide and almost unbroachable. In fact, Wright and Shaw were close contemporaries and fond of each other; early in his career Shaw had a studio in the Loop's Steinway Hall, which also housed early members of the Prairie School. Yet Wright's disdain for Shaw's traditional manor houses was sharp. In a 1918 address entitled "Chicago Culture," Wright declared that architecture ought to reflect social purpose and progress. Shaw, he believed, designed houses for people who preferred stage settings of a classical or Gothic type. In describing one Shaw house he said, "I utterly failed to imagine entering it other than in a costume. . . . I can see it as great fun (very expensive fun), but how can it be seen as culture when the essence of all true culture is a *development* of self-expression?"

If there is a hint of envy in Wright's words it is because Shaw was one of Chicago's most successful residential architects right up until his premature death in 1926, while Wright endured many periods of struggle. Envy, of course, squares with Wright's prickly nature. More specifically, it squares with the fact that one of Wright's greatest disappointments as an architect came as a result of a commission he lost in the spacious suburb of Lake Forest, where Shaw was having such great success. It was the home of Harold McCormick on property overlooking Lake Michigan. Wright designed one of his most dramatic residences ever in about 1907 for the farm-equipment scion and his wife, Edith Rockefeller McCormick. The house itself was pushed up dramatically to the edge of the bluff, and open galleries extended out into the gardens. If it had been built, it might have been the greatest Prairie house ever and might have nudged the barons of business toward modern architecture. It never was. New York architect Charles A. Platt was hired instead. So began the decline of Wright's immediate influence; he left Chicago for Europe shortly thereafter.

Opposite: Chicago Board of Trade, 141 West Jackson Boulevard. Completed 1930, Holabird and Root
Powerful and simple vertical lines characterized big-city architecture in the twenties. The Board of Trade is simpler and more forceful than most buildings of the period and only recently has garnered the credit that it deserves for both its interior and exterior design.

Wright's criticism of Shaw was understandable, but it leaves an overdrawn and mistaken impression. Shaw's houses were traditional in appearance—this being the preference of his wealthy clientele—but they were also attractive because they drew from a set of clearly modern ideas. While Shaw's facades may evoke feudal times, his interiors are remarkably open. Spaces flow and rooms are filled with light—qualities that also characterized the Prairie School. Shaw was a devotee of arts and crafts, and he used leaded glass, carved wood, wrought iron, and sculpture in his houses whenever possible. While his inspiration appears to have come from the remote past, his mastery of interior space and the subtleties of detail in his houses were clearly advanced for the time.

Shaw was described by a fellow Steinway Hall denizen as "the most rebellious of the conservatives, and the most conservative of the rebels." Rebellion does not describe Howard Shaw's gentle nature and his obvious ability to charm his wealthy patrons. Yet from the beginning of his career, he joined other Chicago architects in pushing residential design toward more modern ideas. Like the Prairie School, he believed that a house design must respond to the particular conditions faced by the architect. The process was creative, and the outcome each time was unique. Indeed, Shaw never settled into a formula. Of the dozens of Shaw houses in the Chicago area, each possesses charms that are entirely its own. "Personality is the thing," wrote one of Shaw's many admirers in Western Architect magazine on the occasion of the architect's death. While some might notice only copied historical styles in Shaw's houses, many colleagues saw features that were "idealistic."

Shaw separated himself from the quest for a distinct American style. Many of his houses were inspired instead by the English arts and crafts movement, one that recalled medieval times when craftsmanship, not machines, dominated people's lives. While his Prairie counterparts were bent on harnessing the machine, Shaw's world had little use for it. His roofs were steeply pitched. His windows had shutters and flower boxes. Still, his emphasis on craftsmanship and interior space allied Shaw with the moderns, and through him conservative families who assumed they were living like ancient gentry had homes that were in some ways remarkably modern.

Shaw came from a privileged background. His father was a wealthy dry goods merchant, and there was a line of educated forebears that came from the East. After private high school on Chicago's South Side, Shaw attended Yale University and graduated in the class of 1890. He then enrolled at Massachusetts Institute of Technology for architectural training. Before starting at MIT, Shaw worked for a summer at the office of William Le Baron Jenney in Chicago, but the major's strict utilitarianism seems to have had little effect on him. More important to his education, perhaps, were subsequent travels in England, France, and Italy, where his inveterate sightseeing strengthened his resolve to be an architect. It was in Europe that Shaw saw clearly the creative possibilities inherent in traditional styles. "I wish I might remember everything and have the right idea ready for use; that's the only way a man may become a great architect," he wrote to his new wife while he was in Europe.

When Shaw opened his own practice, initially in the attic of his parents' Chicago home, he was busy almost immediately working for well-to-do clients. He designed Georgian-style town houses in Hyde Park and country estates in Lake Forest. Despite a fondness for manor houses in the English style, he quickly developed a reputation for versatility. "He designs individual houses for particular clients and borrows from anyone or any number of sources as much or as little as he pleases," wrote Architec-

tural Record in 1913. "But wide as is the range of his sources, it has significant limits. He rarely gets too far away from the English renaissance . . . and he will have no dealing with frog-eating Frenchmen. Few contemporary American architects are so entirely free from French influence as he is."

Shaw's freedom of design—especially from French-style formality—earned him a lifetime of praise and prosperity. His flexibility was admired by the critics and, more important, by his clients, who were convinced that they would get a suitable "Italian villa" or a small "Gothic castle" or whatever they wanted by hiring Shaw. A blueblood himself, he understood what charmed his class, and this meant he sent bouquets to clients on move-in day and called upon them when they were settled. If his counterpart Wright was cranky, Shaw was polished. While Wright pushed the limits of architecture, Shaw took originality only so far as circumstances allowed. The result was that he was uncommonly successful. He was never without important commissions, and he even designed two high-rise cooperatives near the lakefront for friends and investors—projects that helped to make him quite wealthy himself.

RAGDALE'S "CULTIVATED SHABBINESS"

The purest version of Shaw's architecture, not surprisingly, is his own Lake Forest home, called Ragdale. Its gables, plain plaster walls, flower boxes, and landscape make the place look like a Hobbit's lair. It was probably the kind of escapist fantasy that made staunch modernists look askance. But in its details we notice something important to the architecture of any age: it was well suited to the individuality of the owner. Ragdale became a kind of "experimental laboratory" to test ideas for design and craftsmanship. Shaw named it Ragdale as a family joke; he had seen a house in England called "Ragdale" and liked its sound of "cultivated shabbiness," the sense that the place was forever unfinished. Besides being designer, Shaw worked there as carpenter, bricklayer, gardener, and painter along with hired hands, and he was never so happy as when he worked in old knickers as a jack-of-all-trades.

Ragdale, 1230 North Greenbay Road, Lake Forest. Completed 1898, Howard Van Doren Shaw
Ragdale was a laboratory for Howard Van Doren Shaw's ideas, many of which drew from the English arts and crafts movement. It was the architect's own house, inspired more by fantasies than true antecedents. Shaw brought to it the repose and dignity that made him a successful architect of stately residences for wealthy clients.

Ragdale

Above: The front hall of Ragdale. A love of modest finishes and love of art characterizes Shaw's approach to his own home in Lake Forest.

Opposite: In the dining room, Shaw held to the arts and crafts idiom of his day—beamed ceiling, plate rail, large pieces of furniture, and glass openings all around.

The hand of the craftsman gives the place a look of studied informality. The entrance hall has woodwork of unpainted oak, and between the hall and the dining room are six large panels of leaded glass. Window seats, Stickley chairs, and Mission oak with pewter inlay are typical of the interior decor. Rusticity prevailed outside as well, but ironically perhaps, the architect left little to chance. Narrow paths were cut through Ragdale's property, which was about fifty acres. Shaw placed English-style signs where paths crossed. The garden has a dovecote, and a sundial is inscribed with verse.

Perhaps the most famous feature of Shaw's home was Ragdale Ring, a small outdoor theater. Plays written by Shaw's wife, Frances, were performed there. Memories are that figures such as Vachel Lindsay, Carl Sandburg, and even William Butler Yeats attended productions at the Ring. These visits are not documented, but their absolute truth is not essential. Ragdale, like much of Shaw's architecture, was designed for the imagination.

DAVID ADLER AND HIS "GREAT HOUSES"

By the end of Shaw's life, his gentle forays into medievalism grew old-fashioned; tastes were moving away from arts and crafts. The 1920s were a glossier and more aggressive age, and the architect who embodied the era, for the upper classes at any rate, was one of Shaw's former draftsmen, David Adler. Adler built traditional residences more vividly and more harmoniously—not to say more extravagantly— than any other architect of his age. He designed lavish town houses, mostly in Chicago but also in New York. His large estates are concentrated around Chicago, but they also grace sites in New England, California, and Hawaii. Modern, Adler was not. Almost always he built in styles that his clients could easily name: "Louis XVI" or "Italianate" or "South African Colonial" became his repertoire. Words like "historical" or "conservative" or "eclectic" aptly describe him, yet even in Adler's work we see the advance of progressive ideas.

Every distinguished architect is a creature of his time, and it is interesting to ponder what characterized Adler's era. Certainly, there was a conservative backlash in the twenties that was brought on by the ugliness of World War I and other troubling signs in Europe. It is no coincidence that Adler's architecture followed a world shaken by Bolshevism in Europe; his homes recalled times that were kinder to aristocrats. It was a revival that was short-lived, as Adler himself admitted when he was elected to the National Institute of Arts and Letters in 1945. Asked to characterize his architecture, Adler said, "My work is all in the period of the 'great house,' which today, alas, is over." Great house implies English; he was equally enchanted with Italian villas and French châteaux.

One of the mysteries of David Adler (no relation to Dankmar Adler) is how the quiet but rebellious person that he was became one of the most intensely conservative architects of his generation. Adler was born to prosperous parents in Milwaukee. He went to Lawrenceville School and then to Princeton University, where he graduated in 1904. Then he embarked for Europe and enrolled in the architecture program at the Munich Polytechnikum. For reasons unknown, he finished three half-year semesters but failed to complete the curriculum to receive his diploma. Later he enrolled in the Ecole des Beaux-Arts in Paris, where he completed his classwork but declined to complete the required thesis for his diploma. No one knows what prevented Adler from doing what was necessary to receive credentials. Even after he began his successful practice in Chicago, he remained unlicensed in Illinois, and his partners had to sign plans that were prepared in his office. In one apparently perfunctory attempt to pass the state exam, he answered a test question about roof structure by writing: "I have men in my

Ryerson Residence, 1406 North Astor Street. Completed 1921, David Adler

Adler chose a Louis XVI style for the Ryersons, whose fortune came from steel. While it is entirely traditional, the architect studiously filled the rooms with natural light and otherwise suited the modern needs of his clients as well as their conventional tastes.

Ryerson Residence
The model for this staircase was from a different age, but its execution demonstrates that Adler and his clients were being influenced by the modern taste for simplicity as well as the desire to be connected with a more noble time and place.

office who take care of that sort of thing." He failed dismally, though later in his career he was able to pass and get a proper license.

What Adler did have was the most uncanny appreciation and eye for design. When he traveled in Europe, he collected hundreds of postcards of houses he admired, and he kept and used them for reference throughout his career. On the backs of these cards he often drew moldings, windows, doors, and other details. He copied, but he was not a plagiarist. Draftsmen in Adler's office were often mystified by Adler's ability to replicate the forms of past architects with exactitude, yet come up with something that was his own. "Adler's extreme care in selecting details from architectural documents bordered on the creative," one of his employees said. He understood how a window or door from a worthy French or Early American model could be combined gracefully with elements in other styles if all were proportioned with utter precision.

Ryerson Residence
This oval-shaped dining room represents a perfectly proportioned Adler interior. It is ornate but uncluttered, and the space achieves the feel of a much larger room than this one really is.

While his sense of detail may have bordered on the creative, his methods of work bordered on the eccentric. Working drawings produced by his office were often done in full scale, which could fill his studio with oceans of paper. This peculiar custom was motivated by Adler's absolute insistence on perfection—and presumably his lack of confidence in carpenters and plastermen to interpret conventionally scaled drawings. Adler was a horrendous draftsman himself and probably never touched a saw or chisel, but he noticed instantly if finished work was off by even the smallest fraction. He would walk into new construction, point to a slight flaw in a cornice, and order it torn down. It was a superhuman eye and was "scary," says Paul Schweikher, who worked for Adler and became a dean of the Yale School of Architecture. Schweikher, whose own residential designs were unabashedly modern, said that he learned his unshakeable sense of proportion from David Adler.

Proportion clearly is the lesson of the Ryerson House, built in 1921 on Astor Street in Chicago. The motif is French—Louis XVI—and was rigorously followed throughout. What is striking about the interior is its light touch and restraint in a style that could easily become decadent. Modern taste was seeping in. Adler designed the Ryersons' grand staircase, for example, in keeping with the French original but elegantly streamlined it as well. His understanding of geometry and proportion was such that he deftly added new touches to old models—such as unique stainless steel patterns in ebony floors—and he blended them without trouble into a set that could have otherwise served the grandest costume drama.

There is no argument but that Adler's styles are anachronisms. Yet his architecture shows that he understood and applied the lessons of organic architecture. In the William McCormick Blair House, built in 1926 in the North Shore suburb of Lake Bluff, his clients wanted an informal home that would take advantage of the breezes coming off Lake Michigan. To accommodate them, Adler devised a floor plan that is never more than one room deep. Air circulates freely, and each room brings in sunlight from two and often three sides. To suit the layout, Adler chose an eighteenth-century colonial "New Netherlands" style, historically asymmetrical because such houses began as cottages and grew with the addition of new rooms over time, a strikingly creative choice under the circumstances. The eighteenth-century dining room with painted Delft tiles—modeled after a room in the American Wing at New York's Metropolitan Museum—blends with a living room of pine paneling, transported in its entirety from a colonial house in Virginia. Adler designed other rooms from his imagination, defining a homelike touch or a formal one by a particular type of molding or finish of tiles. Blair House is a place of varied spaces and feelings, which all flow together harmoniously because of Adler's genius for drawing from memory and adapting the details to perfect scale.

William McCormick Blair House, Lake Bluff. Completed 1926, David Adler

Opposite, above: Mr. Blair wanted a house that would take maximum advantage of the breezes off Lake Michigan. Adler followed the model of an eighteenth-century "New Netherlands" house, a cottagelike structure with a series of sections that were rarely more than one-room deep. In the authentic vernacular style, such houses could be rambling, but Adler's design was a harmonious blend of American colonial motifs.

Opposite, below: Adler's memory for architectural detail, drawn from his frequent travels to the East and Europe, enabled him to combine varied elements and create rooms that appeared historical but were in fact entirely original.

Below: Blair House features an indoor tennis court with a lofty steel superstructure and topiary eagles reaching toward the sky.

William McCormick Blair House

Above: Spaces in the Blair home flow seamlessly due to Adler's almost amazing sense of proportion for moldings, paneling, and other features.

Below: A guest bedroom in Blair House.

As the 1920s progressed, some of the same conditions that spawned Adler's "great house" era also brought in persuasive modern notes. The twenties were a time of expanding wealth, renewed optimism, and frequent travel abroad for pleasure. During this time, American architects and clients were exposed to many new and modern styles. The most instantly appealing of these was Art Deco, characterized by glossy, colorful finishes that became popular due to the Exposition Internationale des Arts Décoratifs et Industriels Modernes in Paris in 1925.

Modern European design cast an influence on America initially through interiors. It was a simple and private matter for clients to renovate apartments or commercial spaces in ways that some might find daring or peculiar. Before long, however, modernism took on a more public role and quickly influenced the outside face of architecture in cities around the country. In downtown Chicago, the 1920s began with skyscrapers fashioned in the classical and Gothic styles, but the decade ended with streamlined towers resembling the skyline of Clark Kent's Metropolis.

Modernism was not accepted without argument. As late as 1927 Chicago's Association of Arts and Industries sponsored a debate at the Palmer House on the topic: "Resolved, That the hope of art expression lies in the modern movement." Speaking for the conservatives was Miss Marion Gheen, an interior decorator with a wealthy clientele and an office on Ontario Street. "Every true artist, in working out the impulse to create that which mysteriously rises within him, is bound to revert to the use of classic forms," she said.

On the modern side was Alphonso Ianelli, a noted sculptor and teacher at the Art Institute of Chicago. Classical art was exhausted, Ianelli declared. "It is as silly for us to build our Field Museum, stadium, and aquarium in classic Greek architectural style as it would be for us to issue our daily newspapers in the language of classic Greece." The view was not particularly new; it went back to the days of Louis Sullivan. But now, Ianelli insisted, modern design was taking hold in store windows, in sleek automobiles, and other areas, even among people who considered modern art "weird."

Following pages, left: Chicago Tribune Tower competition entries, unbuilt, 1922
Above left: Eliel Saarinen
Saarinen's entry in the Chicago Tribune's competition to design "the most beautiful and distinctive office building in the world" was awarded second place. Though it was not built, the design was the most influential of the 263 entries. With historical touches and proud vertical thrust, it was viewed as a monument to America's vision and power.
Above right: Adolf Loos
Loos was an avant-garde architect from Vienna, where strict classical forms were emphatically out of fashion. For that reason, his entry was viewed by many as a satire on America, whose architects at this time were often tied to historical decoration on modern skyscrapers. There is no evidence that Loos's column design was taken seriously by Colonel Robert R. McCormick, the Tribune's conservative publisher and final arbiter in the competition.
Below left: Walter Gropius and Adolf Meyer
Gropius, founder of the Bauhaus, and other Germans in the early twenties were rediscovering the work of the Chicago School. This tower would have been reinforced concrete—not a steel-frame building—but the design eschewed decoration as did William Le Baron Jenney at his best.
Below right: Holabird and Roche
The canon for skyscrapers at the time was for powerful and sober structures surmounted by towers to be admired from afar. Holabird and Roche showed little restraint in creating something that looked like a Gothic cathedral in the sky.
Following pages, right: Chicago Tribune Tower, 435 North Michigan Avenue. Completed 1925, Hood and Howells
The winning entry was controversial. Architect Alfred Granger, a member of the jury, likened it to a live creature with "flesh and muscles" covering a fine skeleton. Louis Sullivan, by then a bitter man, called it architecture "evolved of dying ideas."

Modernism eventually took hold in the large-scale projects, but again, not without battles. One of the central episodes of twentieth-century architecture, the Tribune Tower competition, made Chicago the center of this debate. The competition and its controversial outcome became a touchstone for modernists for years to come. It began in 1922, when the *Chicago Tribune*, the city's oldest and largest newspaper, announced a design competition for "the most beautiful and distinctive office building in the world." The prize money was $100,000 in all, with $50,000 and the commission going to the first-place design. The *Tribune* advertised the competition internationally and attracted 263 entries. The design that won was by Hood and Howells, a New York firm (which reportedly employed a relative of *Tribune* publisher Colonel Robert R. McCormick, adding fuel to the ensuing controversy). But the truly influential design of the competition was by the second-place finisher, Eliel Saarinen, a successful Finnish architect who would later distinguish himself in America.

A sort of permanent dispute has arisen about the relative merits of the first- and second-place designs for the Tribune Tower. Even today some people prefer the ornate Gothic tower that Colonel McCormick eventually built. Others prefer the Saarinen design. Some historians wonder why the *Tribune* all but ignored entries from such well-known European modernists as Walter Gropius, whose entry foreshadowed the steel and glass towers that would rise in Chicago a generation later. As for the continuing controversy over the Tribune Tower competition, architectural historian Carl W. Condit sums it up as well as anyone: "The first-prize design will very likely continue to be a matter of controversy on through the years; one can only say that the jurors could have done far worse in selecting the winner and that their scorn for the modern style was unfortunately borne out by the undistinguished work that the modernists submitted."

The Tribune Tower jury surprised no one at the time by choosing the historical Gothic skyscraper of Hood and Howells. It was the early twenties, and historical eclecticism (designs that copied models from past eras) was a hard fashion to overcome. Ever since the Columbian Exposition, tall buildings in Chicago typically followed the proportions and interior construction of the utilitarian Chicago School, but most were covered top to bottom with classical pediments and scrolls. Later, New York's Woolworth Building, built in 1913, demonstrated that Gothic motifs provided a gracefully lofty form for skyscrapers and also satisfied America's craving for history. Under these circumstances, the Hood and Howells Tribune Tower entry was impressive: "The steel is covered as in the skeleton of the human body, but, while the covering, like the flesh and muscles, satisfies the eye, the frame always makes its presence felt through the covering," wrote architect Alfred Granger, who was on the Tribune jury.

The "flesh and muscles" simile may have been coined for those speaking the language of organic architecture, but it did not convince the originator of the concept, Louis Sullivan, who was still living and writing at the time. Sullivan wrote an essay on the Tribune competition for *Architectural Record* in 1923 and compared the flying buttresses around Hood and Howells's upper stories to "the monster on top with its great longlegs reaching far below to the ground." Sullivan acknowledges that this building, without its intricate decoration atop, is a "rather amiable and delicate affair with a certain grace of fancy." Sullivan was a deeply bitter man when he wrote this essay, and the competition epitomized his own failed world. "The first prize is demoted

1301 North Astor
The lobby of 1301 North Astor is classically proportioned but modernistically finished with terrazzo floors, stylized furniture, and the streamlined look of the time.

to the level of those works evolved of dying ideas," he writes. "It looks also like the wandering of a mind unaccustomed to distinguish between architecture and scene painting." Sullivan voluntarily cut short his blazing critique partly because "it is cruel to go on, for analysis is now becoming vivisection." He was equally intent on praising Saarinen's entry, which he admired as fervently as he deplored the first.

Saarinen's tower was a truly inventive design, reminiscent of something Gothic but stripped of added decoration. It is proper to place this tower midway between the historicist American entries and the modernist Europeans. To Sullivan, Saarinen had combined the romance of the past with the thrusting power of modern urban culture. He wrote that "the Finlander . . . grasped the intricate problem of the lofty steel-framed structure, the significance of its origins, and held the solution unwaveringly in mind, in such wise as no American architect has as yet shown the required depth of thought and steadfastness of purpose to achieve." Indeed, Saarinen's tower copied no style. Its structure underneath was highlighted with simple and powerful piers that soared skyward as if to defy gravity. Put another way, it was Sullivanesque, a word that can be used to describe many modern skyscrapers of the twenties. Saarinen's design, though not built, was widely published and far more influential than the tower that stands today. It prompted him to leave his country the following year and embark on an eminently successful practice in America, his most famous commission being the Cranbrook Academy of Art in Michigan, where he also taught.

The term "Sullivanesque" refers primarily to the modern tendency to design powerful, nonhistorical skyscrapers. Other aspects of modernism in the later 1920s might have pleased Louis Sullivan considerably less. Modernism was used by some designers not to promote the spirit of American democracy but to create settings for fashionable living. A progressive modern spirit may have inspired the Art Deco movement when it was introduced in France—its sleek lines and polychromed finishes celebrated the populist machine age. Yet America quickly adopted the style, also called Art Moderne and "streamlined," as high fashion. Art Deco crossed the Atlantic in large measure via ocean liners that decorated themselves in bedazzling geometric designs and glimmering colors.

As these and other new ideas floated in, a number of Chicago designers experimented with their possibilities. Among the most important was Robert Switzer, formerly of the interiors department at Holabird and Roche. Switzer and his partner Harold O. Warner opened a shop in 1927 called Secession, Ltd., on Dearborn Street, which specialized in modern decorative arts, including the more restrained styles from Germany and Austria. Switzer and Warner had traveled in Europe earlier that year to study museums in preparation for a renovation of the Art Institute. They apparently paid more attention to the furniture they encountered en route and bought up so much of it, Switzer later said, that they had to open a shop to recover their investment. This they did by finding clients flush with money and anxious to replace their tired classical or antique interiors with something colorful, fresh, and new.

Another key figure of the period was Philip Maher, son of the Prairie architect George Washington Maher. A sign of the Jazz Age was that fashionable stores became social gathering places. To maintain the custom, retailers frequently called on modern architects to redesign their interiors. One of Philip Maher's more famous commissions of the twenties was Stanley Korshak's Blackstone Shop on Michigan Avenue, which sold ladies' couture. Before beginning the renovation, Korshak took Maher to New York City to see Bergdorf Goodman, one of the nation's most fashionable stores, and to look at the ocean liner *Isle de France*, a famous Art Deco extravaganza. The Blackstone Shop opened in 1929. The design was restrained, perhaps, but definitely modern. It was light in color and feel; the furniture was reminiscent of eighteenth-century French pieces but had sleek lines and smooth surfaces. This look became typical of the era and in its various forms insinuated itself into the most respectable parlors.

GRAHAM, ANDERSON, PROBST AND WHITE

Chicago's bastion of traditional architecture in the 1920s was the firm of Graham, Anderson, Probst and White, a successor to Daniel Burnham and Company. Graham, Anderson, as it was called, was wealthy and enjoyed excellent political connections. The story of its leading member, Ernest R. Graham, goes back to the construction of the 1893 World's Columbian Exposition, where as Burnham's young factotum he rode the grounds on a white horse and issued orders to everyone in sight. Graham became heir-apparent to the firm, not because he was a designer of talent, but because he was savvy about business and good with monied clients. Early in his career, Graham himself grew rich by making personal investments in commercial buildings that the Burnham firm designed and built.

An architectural enterprise could hardly have been more conservative than Graham, Anderson. After it completed the new Straus Building on South Michigan Avenue (an eclectic classical skyscraper later sold to CNA Insurance Companies), architect Andrew Rebori wrote in a 1925 issue of *Architectural Record*: "Those entrusted with the design and execution of this huge structure were never once swayed by the emotion of the creative mind. They followed along the smooth path of accepted precedent. . . . The result is massive impressiveness." Nevertheless, this firm was nothing if not a creature of its place and time, and as modern ideas became acceptable, Graham, Anderson responded.

The liberties the firm took with classical precedent naturally occurred in interior space earlier than on the exteriors of their buildings. Outside, a Graham, Anderson commission could resemble a structure from ancient Greece or Rome. But inside there was often a vastness that harked back directly to Chicago—Root's Rookery, for instance, or Burnham's Railway Exchange. Other notes of modern design took more time to penetrate this most traditional of firms, but when they came in the mid-1920s, they served as irrevocable proof that the architectural world had changed. Graham, Anderson's Field Museum, built in 1921, could hardly be more staid both inside and out; its exterior is entirely Greek and its interior is as reposed and colorless as the white marble outside. The following year the firm showed some drift toward the modern in the Continental Bank Building, which outside, on LaSalle Street, had the customary classical lines. What was added inside was color. Murals high above the floor of the main banking room were executed by Jules Guerin, best known for his atmospheric watercolors illustrating Burnham's 1909 *Plan of Chicago*. Guerin was the director of color for the 1915 Panama-Pacific International Exposition, "a classical city ablaze with the colors of the Mediterranean"—in absolute contrast to Chicago's White City in 1893. The bank murals, depicting commerce around the world, do not verge on anything like the social realism that would decorate many buildings a few years hence. His compositions were self-contained and quiet. Yet Guerin's interest in color is early evidence that Graham, Anderson was ready to move from staid classicism and into the modern era.

And modern, indeed, was Graham, Anderson's Merchandise Mart, which was built as a grand and utterly new concept. Completed in 1930, the Mart would be the world's largest building and the latest word in consolidating wholesalers from throughout the Midwest in one place. This called for a definitely modern look, for which this most conservative of firms borrowed, ironically perhaps, from the nineteenth century—the warehouses of the Chicago School. Blocklike and big shouldered, the Merchandise Mart is as structural and utilitarian as old Chicago itself. Elegantly proportioned and bathed at night in warm spotlights—showing off true Art Deco lines—it could have been the warehouse from Oz. And modernity applied inside as well as out. Interior detail was squared off and abrupt. There was color everywhere. The Art Moderne barber shop was a "Busby Berkeley extravaganza of musical chairs," as described by Sally Anderson Chappell in a recent book on Graham, Anderson, Probst and White.

The final modernization of Graham, Anderson, Probst and White came during the depression with the Field Building on LaSalle Street (on the site of Jenney's Home Insurance Building). Here the firm broke emphatically with its traditional past. The jazzy, modern world had arrived, and the firm designed a stripped-down, streamlined skyscraper, thrusting skyward in a way that can easily be termed Sullivanesque. Graham, Anderson's modern design for the Field Building was hardly whimsical. Real estate brochures printed for its opening advertised what mattered to the market when the building was completed in 1934. It had all the up-to-date amenities: high-speed

Above and following pages: Merchandise Mart, between Wells and Orleans streets at the Chicago River. Completed 1930, Graham, Anderson, Probst and White

When it was built, the Merchandise Mart was the world's largest building. It inaugurated this conservative firm's foray into pronounced modernism. At night, bathed in spotlights, the Mart might have seemed like the Chicago School warehouse from Oz. It has 250,000 square feet per floor. It was designed with proportions that were classical but also with the angularity that typified the Art Deco period. Plain geometric form combined with rich finishes—these qualities characterized Graham, Anderson, Probst and White's short, happy period as proponents of the streamlined style.

Field Building (now LaSalle National Bank Building), 135 South LaSalle Street. Completed 1934, Graham, Anderson, Probst and White

Opposite: Graham, Anderson, Probst and White confirmed its modern tendencies with the Field Building, which has been called "Sullivanesque" for the strong vertical thrust of its exterior.

Above: Graham, Anderson, Probst and White's brief career in Art Deco modernism (the depression cut it short), the fluted columns of the Field Building are elongated and abstract. The office building was the firm's contribution to the Jazz Age on LaSalle Street.

Following page: Glossy surfaces and bold geometric forms characterize the Field Building lobby, stylistically Art Deco or Moderne but with a sure sense of classical proportion that was so important to the firm's previous designs.

elevators, for example, and alternating current for better radio reception. Its large and dramatic lobby had walkways suspended overhead—reminiscent of the Rookery across the street but streamlined with decoration that came from the most modern trains, boats, and planes. It was a building for people on the move.

"ARISTOCRATIC" MODERNISM: HOLABIRD AND ROOT

The most emphatic modern architecture of downtown Chicago in this era was designed by a firm whose pedigree went back to the beginning of the Chicago School. In 1928, Holabird and Roche became Holabird and Root, changed for John Wellborn Root, Jr., son of the first Root, who had been a member of the Holabird firm for fourteen years. The name change came simultaneously with some of the finest modern buildings in the country at the time. Holabird and Roche had been for some years a conservative firm. Holabird and Root immediately distinguished itself for a series of buildings that were strikingly progressive inside and out. This firm was hardly teeming with radicals. Rather, its method was collaborative. It incorporated the work of the best professionals it could find in interior design, sculpture, mural painting, and even landscape architecture. Under such circumstances, new ideas rapidly crystallized and flourished.

Holabird and Root is best known today for the Chicago Board of Trade, completed in 1930 and a tour de force influenced, no doubt, by Saarinen's Tribune Tower entry.

Chicago Board of Trade

In the Chicago Board of Trade, "ziggurats" were inspired by a fascination with ancient Egypt and by the setbacks that were fashionable in the exterior design of modern skyscrapers. Translucent glass, nickel reflectors, and seven varieties of marble contribute to a lobby that is a model of Art Deco streamlining.

"Every inch a proud and soaring thing," reported *Architecture Magazine* in February 1932. The forty-four-story building shunned tradition in many ways. Its skyward thrust and setbacks resembled the setback style, which became popular first in Manhattan, where zoning laws prohibited sheer vertical walls that darkened city streets. The Board of Trade could be floodlit at night to emphasize its strong modern form. On top, the sculpture of Ceres, goddess of grain, was unabashedly Art Deco. Inside, the lobby's polychromed effects, with chevrons and zigzags, were inspired partially by Egyptian forms made popular by the sensational discovery of Tutankhamen's tomb a few years before. Lamps were hidden behind translucent glass, and nickel reflectors helped diffuse indirect light, a relatively new technique. Gold leaf and faience were added for brightness, even flash, in a design that owed little to precedent.

Another Holabird and Root building, known only as 333 North Michigan Avenue, is often overlooked but remains one of America's great modern buildings of the twenties. Carl W. Condit called it "aristocratic," which is an apt label because it was highly influential not only for its bold style but also for its financial success. So prestigious was 333 that Holabird and Root themselves took offices there along with several other large architectural firms. Outside, its lines are powerful yet gentle and owe obvious debts to Saarinen's Tribune Tower and many designs of earlier vintage. Its long and narrow floor plate—assuring ample light for all tenants—takes its lesson from the old Monadnock Building, and well it should. John Root, Sr., designed the Monadnock, and its later addition was by Holabird and Roche.

If the exterior of 333 was stately, its interior, also by Holabird and Root, reveals, on the brink of the depression, the epitome of modern. It was the Tavern Club, an Art Deco drinking establishment for any member who has "ever done any thing, or thought any thing and is of a clubable nature," according to the club's bylaws. John Root, a member, said that its purpose was "to create an environment in which it might be possible to escape from the pressures of the moment by having one's thought directed in the direction of the future rather than the past." The Tavern Club's interior design had nothing to do with old oak paneling and moose heads. Instead, it featured murals by John Norton entitled *Pagan Paradise*, a composition of tropical plants and nudes. Furnishings and accents were in pale green, flamingo pink, and jet black. Not everyone approved, of course. One member recalled that some old writers, "rugged followers of the Carl Sandburg tradition," wondered about such a club when they saw it. "The place looks like a milliner's shop," said one grizzled scribe who was probably more accustomed to barrooms with sawdust on the floor.

The Great Depression that followed on the heels of these new buildings drained many people of optimism, but it did not eliminate style. As if creative retailing was the antidote to bad economic times, it is appropriate that one of Chicago's most fondly remembered buildings, Michigan Square Building (also called Diana Court), was completed in 1930 on North Michigan Avenue. Designed by Holabird and Root, it was an enclosed arcade and shopping mall (bringing the Rookery to mind as well as the much later Water Tower Place) decorated throughout with polished metalwork and marble. The famous Swedish sculptor Carl Milles was commissioned to create a sculpture of Diana for the atrium, and tenants were encouraged to design their own storefronts. "Art Moderne dominates the center portion of the building in a motif that sets Michigan Square apart as truly unusual," a building trades magazine reported shortly after it opened. "Holabird and Root, architects of the building, are to be congratulated for having made a fine contribution to the fusion of art and business."

This outstanding building flourished through the depression, but alas, it did not survive. *Chicago Daily News* art critic Dennis Adrian reported on its sad demise in

333 North Michigan Avenue. Completed 1928, Holabird and Root

It soars skyward much like Saarinen's Tribune Tower design. Streamlined and modern, 333 also recalls the old Monadnock with a floor plate that is long and narrow, filling its duly modern interior with plenty of natural light.

1973. "The vandalizing of N. Michigan Ave., or what is left of it, proceeds apace. The most recent loss is the beautiful Michigan Square Building, now being wrecked behind a web of scaffolding." Adrian described the "flying staircases that gave a startling effect of suspension . . . and created wonderfully theatrical effect." Unfortunately, the importance of Diana Court went unappreciated until it was too late to save it. "It would have been a wonderful place to dance," Adrian wrote, which applies to many of Chicago's fine urban buildings from an era that is too often forgotten.

Michigan Square Building (Diana Court), 540 North Michigan Avenue. Completed 1930, demolished 1973; Holabird and Root

Above: A classical sense of proportion underlies the unmistakably modernistic facade of Diana Court, which was widely praised for being a successful synthesis of business and art.

Opposite, below left: Diana Court was the Art Deco jewel of Chicago, demolished in the 1970s before the real-estate moguls knew what they were losing. Its interior shopping mall harked back to the Rookery and presaged Water Tower Place. Its sense of color and original form were unsurpassed by anything seen before or since.

Above left: Diana Court was a center for design shops and other purveyors to the fashion set, lively in Chicago despite the depression.

Above right and below right: Holabird and Root envisioned individuality in the storefronts of Diana Court, so merchants were encouraged to design their own. This strategy paid off. Although Diana Court opened with the depression, store owners believed that a high-fashion image might capture the shrinking clientele for high-end goods. This was the Socatch bake shop, selling rich pastries in hard times.

CHAPTER FIVE

"Less is more." The phrase is inseparable from the architect who uttered it, Ludwig Mies van der Rohe. The phrase is also misleading. The glass and steel architecture of Mies van der Rohe may be "minimalist," but as a distillation of ideas ranging from philosopher Saint Thomas Aquinas to painter Pablo Picasso, there is nothing sparse about it. Robert Venturi trivialized Mies's phrase with a parody: "Less is a bore," he writes in *Complexity and Contradiction in Architecture*. Venturi's satire is an unfortunate misunderstanding because spending time in a Mies van der Rohe space is a rich architectural experience. Learning about what motivated the architect touches on many timeless lessons of architecture.

The German-born Mies was frequently misunderstood and still is. One misunderstanding that has become instructive, however, crossed the friendship between Mies and Frank Lloyd Wright and sheds light on the personalities of both men. Mies settled in Chicago in 1938 but was aware of Wright's work as far back as 1911, when it was published in a lavish portfolio by the prestigious Wasmuth Press of Berlin. Wright possibly knew of Mies in the twenties but certainly became familiar with his work in 1932 with the International style exhibition at the Museum of Modern Art in New York.

The two met in 1937 when Mies was planning his permanent move to America. The German was in Chicago, and Wright was phoned by a mutual acquaintance and told that Mies would like to meet him. "I should think he would," was Wright's inimitable reply. Although Wright cut other European architects off at the knees—he was horrifyingly rude when Walter Gropius attempted to pay his respects—he genuinely admired Mies and invited him to Wisconsin. A visit of a few hours was extended to days. They motored to Racine to witness construction on Wright's Johnson Wax Building, then to Chicago and its suburbs to see Robie House, Coonley House, and Unity Temple.

Mies was clearly impressed. There is no doubt that his conception of space and his reverence for materials was influenced at least partly by Wright's Prairie architecture. Later Mies wrote a short essay for a catalogue that was never published but was intended to accompany a 1940 exhibition of Wright's work at New York's Museum of Modern Art: "Here, finally, was a master-builder drawing upon the veritable fountainhead of architecture; who with true originality lifted his creations into the light."

Architectural egos being what they are, sparks can fly unexpectedly. And fly they did, rather civilly at first by Wright's normal standards, after a 1946 retrospective of Mies's work at MOMA. Wright swept into the opening of the exhibition with more than average pomp, according to one recollection. "Wright was pointing at Mies's work and saying things like, 'I did this in 1925,'" said Joe Fujikawa, a student and employee of Mies at the time. "He was giving everyone the impression that he was behind everything Mies had ever done." Wright must have felt a pang of remorse afterward, for he wrote a letter of explanation—not really an apology—to Mies and invited him for a return visit to Taliesin. Mies wrote back politely that it didn't matter, and he would

Opposite: Design for a Glass Skyscraper, 1922, Ludwig Mies van der Rohe
Mies's fascination with structural steel and glass began early. He designed this skyscraper for Berlin at a time when it had little chance of being built. But the glimmering modernist tower pointed toward what was to come and cast a backward glance to steel-frame, big-window skyscrapers of the Chicago School.

of course be glad to make the trip and talk amiably about architecture. But Mies, who became known for the aphorism "Build, don't talk," never went. Wright apparently regarded this as a snub and later took a shot at Mies's "internationalism," equating it with communism. Both movements, he suggested, must destroy in order to create—"do this very leveling in the name of civilization," as Wright put it. Mies, typically, remained unruffled, but he never saw or communicated with Wright again.

Despite the bad ending, the artistic connection between Mies and Wright goes deep, especially in the way they planned space. Mies's debt to Wright can be overstated, as it was by Wright, but many modern house designs he turned out early in his career feature something very much akin to Wright's interpenetrating space and the dissolving of boundaries between interior and exterior. One 1924 project that Mies designed but never built, the Brick Country House, contains a pattern of free-standing walls that articulate a series of spaces inside. The house was to have glass partitions, exterior courtyards, and brick walls that extended out into the countryside. It clearly appears to be influenced by the Prairie style.

THE ABSTRACT THEORIST

Beyond Wright, other influences on Mies were impressive for their wide range. One important set of ideas came to the architect from the *de Stijl* group, composed mostly of Dutch painters whose art concentrated on the organization of rectilinear lines and primary colors. After the devastation of World War I, the rosy world of Impressionism and post-Impressionism lost its appeal for many artists. The theories of *de Stijl* sought to cleanse art of historical references and reduce it to pure geometric form. The theory of *de Stijl* was influential and is clearly evident in the floor plans of the Brick Country House and other designs by Mies while he lived in Europe.

Another specific influence on the architecture of Mies was the philosophy of Saint Thomas Aquinas, though the architect was far from religious in any conventional sense. Aquinas wrote in the thirteenth century that the spiritual world could be discerned by the observation of things that were visible. Through serious contemplation, human beings could understand the essence of a rock, a blade of grass, or any physical form. The idea that a thing as seemingly inanimate as a steel post or sheet of glass had spiritual impact was an attractive concept to an architect. Mies struggled mightily to assemble the materials of his structures according to their essences. The minimalism of Mies derived from the fact that these essences, when truly captured, neither required nor wanted added decoration.

Mies was an extremely abstract thinker. This was due in some measure to the fact that his maturity as an architect occurred directly after World War I, when the German economy was in near ruin and there was little actual building to do. In this environment it was natural for a serious architect to become something of a theorist, and Mies associated himself with a number of progressive artistic collectives in Berlin. He participated in and even helped organize avant-garde exhibitions where he showed

Opposite: The Arts Club, 109 East Ontario Street. Completed 1951, Ludwig Mies van der Rohe
Above: The Arts Club was designed by Mies for a preexisting building, and furniture that the club already owned would also be used. Mies's charge was to create a gallery space, dining room, and lecture hall. The outcome was a masterpiece of proportion and flowing space. While this stairway in the club's entrance was a design challenge for its size and height, the outcome demonstrates how Mies saw a harmonious solution for any problem.
Below: Galleries were favorite commissions for Mies, since he had designed many exhibitions as a young man. Here he takes advantage of Constantine Brancusi's *Golden Bird*, which once belonged to the club and now is on exhibit at the Art Institute of Chicago.

his experimental designs and won considerable acclaim. One such project was his Glass Skyscraper. Few buildings had any chance at all of being built at this time, 1922, and for that reason Mies blithely advanced this alarmingly radical concept: a steel skeleton exposed beneath transparent walls of glass. The connection between this building and the earlier steel frames and large windows of the Chicago School is inescapable, though Mies might have described his tower in Thomist terms abstract enough to leave most practical Americans quite baffled.

Mies and his compatriots argued endlessly over the small points of their work and ideas. He did not particularly enjoy debate, but he entered into it as the only way an architect could draw notice during Germany's dreadful economic slump. He formed relationships with Constructivists, a group of Russian designers then working in Berlin who saw their unemotional task as "not to decorate life but to organize it." Mies frequently published articles in magazines explaining what became known as the New Architecture. "We reject all aesthetic speculation, all doctrine, all formalism," he wrote in prose that was as spare as his architecture. "We refuse to recognize problems of form, but only problems of building." And he continued to display visionary drawings at exhibitions. His reputation grew, and when the economy recovered enough for building in Germany to begin again, Mies headed the list of eligible architects. The New Architecture was criticized, to be sure, by conservatives. But the effect even of the attacks was increased exposure, and commissions came his way.

IS MIES LIVABLE?

The Barcelona Pavilion, or more properly the German Pavilion, at the 1928 world's fair in Barcelona, Spain, gave Mies a chance to demonstrate his ideas in a design that was more a large-scale sculpture than a building constructed for a useful purpose. It was intended as a showplace for Germany's building-supplies industry, and Mies's only mandate was to show the products to their best possible advantage. Under a flat roof, the pavilion was filled with free-standing walls, flowing space, and sensations enhanced by the rich materials. It had giant slabs of polished onyx, thick wool rugs, and travertine floors that extended to the edge of a limpid pool in the rear. Most important, perhaps, was something relatively new at the time—great walls of glass all around. The use of glass was important to the New Architecture for theoretical reasons as well as practical ones. Among its interesting qualities, glass enabled architects to reveal interior and exterior space simultaneously and had the added benefit of reflection. This was curious and stimulating—glass enabled architects to merge points of view that used to be separate, achieving in architecture what Picasso and the Cubists were attempting to do in painting. For reasons that have everything to do with Mies's consummate skill at blending abstract ideas with real materials, the Barcelona Pavilion (which was dismantled after the fair and reconstructed in 1986) is remembered as a milestone in architecture. So resolved was every aspect of the design that Mies even designed the furniture, which included the so-called Barcelona chair.

The question remains: Does a great moment in modern art also constitute a suitable, comfortable place in which to live? Mies never answered the question directly but often declared his preference for the ideal over mere bodily comfort. Mies once said that the Barcelona chair was designed for a king, as he knew that Alfonso XIII of Spain would be visiting the pavilion. His idealism on this point was no trivial matter. The day the monarch was due to arrive, Mies was making a last check of his building, and "to my surprise I found a wanderer sitting in the chair. I ordered him out with the following words: 'For you I made a bench outside by the pool.'"

860–880 North Lake Shore Drive. Completed 1952, Ludwig Mies van der Rohe
In designs for 860–880 a few details have changed, but the core of Mies van der Rohe's creation of clean and well-lighted space has not. Design by Powell/Kleinschmidt

860–880 North Lake Shore Drive

Now, as in Mies's own time, basic shapes and basic (though expensive) materials combine to create luxurious settings. The forms are simple but arranged so deftly in the lobby and elsewhere that the skyscrapers of 860–880 seem as fresh and new as they were when they were created more than forty years ago. Design by Powell/Kleinschmidt

Barcelona chair, designed 1929, Ludwig Mies van der Rohe
The chair was first imagined as a throne for the King of Spain. Later it was put into production in Chicago and became a staple for modern interiors.

Less astringent, perhaps, is story of the Tugendhat House, in Brno, Czechoslovakia, completed in 1930. The design is vintage Mies. Its main space, 50 by 80 feet, is enclosed by sheets of glass and partitioned with free-standing onyx walls and an ebony screen. Mies also designed several pieces of furniture for Tugendhat House, a joint effort with his partner during this period, Lilly Reich. Reich deserves much of the credit for the rich fabrics and elegant touches that finished Mies's otherwise stark interiors. Together they left little room in Tugendhat House for non-Miesian elements. All furniture, the piano, and even a sculpture of a female torso were either designed or specified by Mies and Reich.

Critics naturally wondered if the place was not too severe to be livable, and a few negative articles about Tugendhat House showed up in magazines shortly after it was built. As a response, Fritz Tugendhat, Mies's client, took it upon himself to write and publish a defense of his architect in the magazine *Die Form*: "It is true that one cannot hang any pictures in the main space, in the same way that one cannot introduce a piece of furniture that would destroy the stylish uniformity of the original furnishings—but is our 'personal life repressed' for that reason? The incomparable patterning of the marble and the natural graining of the wood do not take the place of art, but rather they participate in the art, in the space, which is here art." Mr. Tugendhat's essay was politically correct, and it had its impact. The fact is, however, that after photographs of the house were taken, the Tugendhats were quick to rearrange things and bring in pieces of their own.

Mies and other Europeans of his time were great idealists, and who can blame them? It was the 1930s, and their society was becoming unhinged. At the same time in America many architects were also going against the traditional grain, but here the terms of the battle were different. American building was ever practical—a lesson not lost on European architects who traveled here to admire skyscrapers and incidentally found strange beauty in grain silos rising from the prairie. Americans also experimented with modernism, and they also used glass. But again the exercise was practical. Minimalist architecture appealed to Americans less because it made them think of modern paintings and more because it seemed to be a way to build buildings quickly and easily, even prefabricate them.

It is not that such architects as George Fred Keck and William Keck—heroes of Chicago modernism—were blind to the philosophical arguments of Mies and the International style. As "machines for living" (this phrase was coined by Le Corbusier), Keck and Keck homes achieved in the thirties a level of innovation that has been matched only rarely since. The Kecks did it by learning about what was new in Europe and keeping the values of old Chicago in mind as well. The Chicago influence attempted to keep construction as quick and economical as possible. Interior spaces should be open and flexible. The Kecks even fought the battle for solar energy, making remarkable strides in the technology before the abundance of cheap energy ruined those efforts after World War II.

Fred Keck, the elder brother and some say the creative genius of the firm, began his architectural career in Chicago in 1921, opening his own practice in 1927. His first commissions were simple, mostly conventional suburban homes for clients brought in by friendly real estate developers. Business was good for a while, but the depression came along and took a quick toll on architects. This, in retrospect, was a kind of blessing. Fred Keck had long wanted to build in a far more modern style, but that was difficult in good times when everything was business as usual. "We had problems getting financing for anything that was modern and up-to-date," says William Keck, Fred's surviving younger brother who joined the firm in 1931.

Depression in the building industry was what enabled the Kecks to build their first truly modern home, the House of Tomorrow at Chicago's Century of Progress Exposition in 1933. Fred Keck's objective in this remarkable house was to show how modern building supplies could be used gracefully and economically. So he asked the makers of glass, steel, rubberized flooring, and dozens of other products to provide materials for what would be a modern showplace. The compact house he designed—which included a hangar for a small biplane—was a hit. Tens of thousands of visitors to the fair came through the house, and since admission was ten cents, the investors (including the Kecks) even made a little money.

To fair goers, the House of Tomorrow might have looked otherworldly, or at least European, but the Kecks could claim that it was really as American as a Model-T. Its plan was modeled after a four-story brick mansion called the Octagon House that the Kecks knew from their youth in Watertown, Wisconsin. The Octagon was built in 1853 with a central core that brought running water from a cistern in the roof and carried

Opposite: Herbert Brunning Residence, Wilmette. Completed 1936, Keck and Keck
This house vividly demonstrates that the Keck method was to conceive interior space and then enclose it with the most suitable and convenient materials available, including glass block, a bold new concept in the thirties.

Herbert Brunning Residence
Simple forms and basic textures formed unique and interesting compositions in the Brunning Residence and in many other houses designed by George Fred Keck and his younger brother, William.

heat from a furnace below. In the Kecks' brochure, which was handed out at the House of Tomorrow, the old Wisconsin house was pictured with commentary: "If the inventive spirit and direct expression as exemplified in this house, built in the middle of the last century, had been carried on, we should have escaped the inanities of the post–Civil War period and the first thirty years of this present century." This brochure goes on to explain that "the chief concern of the architect was not to give a specific form to his building but rather to find a solution to the many and varied new requirements of a residence in a simple and direct manner. The causes were considered first, the effects later. He started from the inside and worked out."

The House of Tomorrow, like the Octagon, had a central core for heating and air conditioning (which "will be considered as necessary as central heating and bathrooms are today," Keck wrote). The plan is a duodecagon, a polygon with twelve equal sides. Not an arbitrary or decorative choice, this was determined to be the most efficient shape for the size of the glass panels to be used. Interior design was eminently uncluttered and intended to preserve the impression of "space and freedom." Furniture and interior finishes were of the simplest form but called attention to themselves by the interesting use of materials. Flooring was of end-grain wood blocks in some cases, bright-colored rubber tile in others. The most influential features of the House of Tomorrow were its chrome-tube furniture and metallic venetian blinds. Convenience became an aesthetic. The Kecks knew that their house would appear strange at first glance, but people would become accustomed to it, even find it "right and proper and beautiful."

As the Century of Progress continued for a second year, the Kecks assembled many of the same suppliers for an encore, the Crystal House, which they hoped would generate as much enthusiasm as the House of Tomorrow. More starkly modern than the previous effort, this one was supported by exterior trusses and enclosed with glass panels, making the interior as open and flexible as possible. The furniture of the Crystal House was designed by the Kecks' talented draftsman Lee Atwood, much of it modeled after pieces he found pictured in publications of Mies's houses in Europe. Unfortunately, the Crystal House did not get the traffic it needed, and the Kecks' personal investment in the project was a loss. "I had to decide between being rich or going for reputation," Fred Keck explained candidly years later. "I was young and built the building and lost my shirt."

After the Century of Progress, Keck and Keck moved in two separate but related directions. One involved designing prefabricated houses that employed solar heating. The other was building fine homes for wealthy and progressive clients.

Fred Keck always said that he discovered the possibilities of solar heat in 1933 quite by accident. The House of Tomorrow was going up in the dead of winter. After the house was enclosed in its glass panels, the tradesmen working inside had to remove their coats because of the radiated heat of the sun. The Kecks were quick to note that the sun's rays could be captured in the design of future houses. They made month-by-month studies of the solar paths so they could orient their houses most advantageously. They designed eaves of the proper width to admit rays in winter and keep them out in summer.

Such ideas were exciting and inexpensive, and shortly after World War II the Kecks joined forces with Rockford, Illinois, developer Edward Green to make and market "Green's Ready-Built Homes." They were attractive prefab jobs, featuring large glass panels facing south and eaves of the correct dimensions. The Kecks modern practical sense also drove them to create an interior that made maximum use of some twenty-five hundred square feet. Built-in dressers and other furniture were strategically placed. Movable partitions could quickly create private bedrooms or open up into large spaces. Scores of Green's houses were built throughout the Midwest in the late forties, but business finally went bad. The reason was that prefabs could not be standardized from place to place—costs and building codes often differed from one town to the next. Solar energy, too, lost its glitter as modern central heating came into vogue, and fossil fuels got inexpensive. In this environment, homebuyers were typically more concerned with initial cost than operating cost. The enterprise folded after a few years, an idea that came and went before its time.

It is fortunate that the Kecks had another set of clients who took a liking to their modern houses. They were not average homeowners; they were wealthy families living in neighborhoods with other houses designed by David Adler and Howard Shaw. In some ways these clients were more unabashedly radical than the Kecks themselves. Among them were Mr. and Mrs. Benjamin J. Cahn, Chicagoans who had property in Lake Forest, where they wanted to build a weekend house. When Mrs. Cahn met the Kecks she told them that she knew about the House of Tomorrow, but what she wanted was different. She wanted "the house of the day after tomorrow."

Actually, Mrs. Cahn had some very special needs. One was that her house required an absolute minimum of upkeep since she was disabled by a hip injury suffered earlier in life. She wanted no curtains, which was easily satisfied because the Kecks were anxious to use exterior venetian blinds. She insisted on no rugs; she got a kind of rubber tile that was soft and easy to maintain. Another requirement was that Mrs. Cahn wanted to be able to sit down any place in the house and read. This was complicated by the fact that she vetoed lamps placed on tables or floors. The Kecks' solution was a

House of Tomorrow, at the Century of Progress, 1933, George Fred Keck

Top: The House of Tomorrow was designed as an exhibit for building-supply industries at the Century of Progress, the world's fair which meant to celebrate in the modernistic world. "The plan of the house is as unusual as it is logical," Keck wrote in a booklet that accompanied the house. Supported by a central steel column, its shape (a twelve-sided polygon) was dictated by the standard size of glass panels that were easy to procure and install.

Left: In the House of Tomorrow, an airplane hangar was logical and relatively simple to include.

Above: Basic forms, simple materials, and natural light combined to create a measure of comfort that most people did not associate with modern design at the time.

Crystal House, at the Century of Progress, 1934, George Fred Keck
For Keck's second futuristic house at the world's fair, interior space was opened entirely by steel trusses on the exterior.

system of pinpoint lights in many places in the ceiling, controlled by discreetly placed switches.

An attractive feature of the Cahn House, which cost in the neighborhood of $125,000 in 1937, was its floor plan, which forms a graceful arc from one end to the other. This is less than strictly utilitarian, but it does serve two specific functions. On the front side a curve in the facade tends to embrace the approaching visitor, providing a warm welcome. In back its sliding glass walls open with maximum views of a Jens Jensen prairie designed for the house that was torn down to make way for this one.

THE INTERIORS OF MARIANNE WILLISCH

With the abundance of new ideas and techniques connected to building, architecture was assuming greater power to improve people's lives. This message came from a variety of places—Wright, Mies, the Kecks. It was particularly true of interiors where experiments were less costly, and for this reason interior designers did much to advance the cause of progressive architecture. A convincing proponent of modernism

Following pages: B. J. Cahn House, Lake Forest. Completed 1938, Keck and Keck
When the Kecks met Mrs. Cahn, she told them she wanted "the house of the day after tomorrow." Space, light, and convenience were her principal requirements for the house, which was to be a weekend retreat from the Cahn's main residence in the city.
Built-in furniture was one way the Kecks made the best use of space. An array of pinpoint lights and ubiquitous ashtrays were placed in the living room so the residents could read and smoke wherever they happened to take a seat. The bedrooms look out on a Jens Jensen-designed prairie planted for the house that once stood on this site.

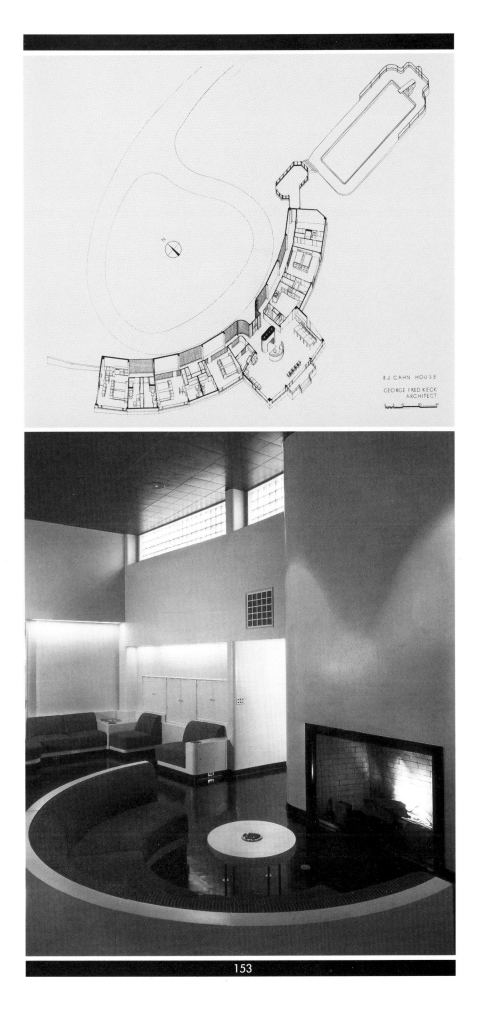

B. J. CAHN HOUSE

GEORGE FRED KECK
ARCHITECT

during this time was Marianne Willisch, a designer who worked closely with the Kecks for many years. Born in Austria, Willisch had been a member of the Werkbund in Vienna, a semi-official design guild with links to the Secession and the Bauhaus. She came to Chicago in 1930 and shortly thereafter opened a design store, Chicago Workshops, in Diana Court. She sold a variety of pieces brought from Europe—Le Corbusier chairs, for example—and also commissioned furniture and decorative pieces that could be made locally. Willisch's shop was not a stirring success and closed after only a few years, but it established her reputation, and she enjoyed a busy design practice ever after.

Willisch's personality was as strong and vivid as her Viennese accent. Interiors, she insisted in an interview shortly before her death in 1984, "should be so organized as to be useful and practical. To do that you have to think not of decorating but of *space planning*." Just as modern structures sought simplicity, so did Willisch's interiors. She acknowledged that she and designers like her endured a "vicious campaign against the Bauhaus, with people saying that the barrenness and coldness of the architecture has spoiled our warm, elegant, and highly decorated interiors." Yet she could boast that many clients left her interiors unchanged for decades, and they remained as fresh and contemporary as when she first designed them. "Taste is only a temporary thing," she said. "Style is organic, and it lasts. It lasts not only to the end of your days but well beyond your lifetime."

Willisch got to know her clients well, saying that she enjoyed the "psychological" aspects of the job. "I will not coerce you," she would protest, but she usually prevailed through insistence on space organization and openness, her absolutes. If the spiel was heavy handed, her designs were not. She liked storage walls because the televisions and stereos they hid were eyesores. Antiques were acceptable in moderation but not "so-called antiques" from junk stores. Fabrics were an important focus, and their textures and colors were often enriched by the play of light.

William Keck remembers Willisch's interiors for "a lot of light . . . light colors. Splashes of colors on the furnishings. Never anything violent at all. Simplicity was her underlying word and underlined doubly." In the many projects they worked on together, Keck remembers only a few times when she was confounded. One was in the Edward McCormick Blair House, built in 1955 in Lake Bluff. Space and furnishings were modern throughout, except that the client insisted on a rather startling rug gotten on a safari in Africa. Willisch objected, but to no avail, and she had to work around the image of a dead animal lying in the middle of her floor.

ANDREW REBORI AND THE FRANK FISHER APARTMENTS

Another important, almost forgotten, architect of the early modern period in Chicago was Andrew Rebori. Born poor in 1886 on New York's Lower East Side, Rebori became a successful and socially prominent architect through force of talent and personality. Rebori spanned social classes, and he spanned eras as well, maintaining his practice well into the 1960s. He was involved in dozens of important buildings from the Art Deco period on. Perhaps his most notable achievement was the Frank Fisher Apartments on Chicago's Near North Side.

Today, with its painted brick and glass block, the Fisher Apartments is a curious, perhaps obscure, piece of "depression modern" architecture. When it was built, however, it demonstrated how much a creative architect could do with new ideas. The project began when client Frank Fisher, an executive of Marshall Field's, presented

Frank Fisher Apartments, 1209 North State Parkway. Completed 1938, Andrew N. Rebori

Interconnecting rooms, balconied lofts, and specially designed furniture enabled Rebori to make the most of apartment spaces, many of which were only 40 feet by 150 feet. Central to Rebori's design were new technologies such as glass block and air conditioning. Rebori also added artistic touches like carving and curious brickwork to mark his buildings with "humanistic logic," which he said softened the mechanisitic spirit of modernism. For his narrow urban lot, client Frank Fisher requested an apartment building with maximum rentable space. Using curves and rounded corners—along with the freedom to devise new forms—Rebori assembled thirteen duplex units that were far more spacious than the exterior would suggest.

Rebori with a long, narrow lot on North State Parkway and asked for a walk-up building with the maximum number of apartments for the space. It was no easy task. The real estate was expensive but the environs were crowded, and whatever else Rebori did, he had to find a way of separating the apartments from the considerable noise of the street. His solution combined an assortment of new and old architectural techniques. They included a light court reminiscent of older Chicago School buildings. They also included the undisguised uses of modern materials that recalled "machines for living," as Le Corbusier called the kinds of dwellings he was designing in Europe.

There was nothing doctrinaire about Rebori's four-story brick building, with thirteen relatively small duplexes. The curvaceous walls were stylish and "moderne" but also practical in the way they brought maximum light into minimal space. Glass block, then in fashion, did much to provide light and privacy. This necessitated another new feature in residential architecture: air conditioning. The otherwise stark exterior was decorated by a large wooden sculpture by artist Edgar Miller, giving the place a touch of vitality and "humanistic logic," as Rebori wrote in a 1937 *Architectural Record* piece shortly after the building was completed. Interiors were organized as a series of interpenetrating spaces, and because of this "telescoping of function," form and color were necessarily simple, as opposed to "the special treatments usually given to rooms designed for a given purpose."

Rebori understood that he was pushing the limits of progressive architecture but that efforts toward the perfect solution were never complete. "From the point of view of what may be termed organic," he wrote, "as contrasted with mere functional mechanisms, it can be said that modern architecture is not yet a reality; it is only a potentiality in the process of being discerned, sought, and practically and occasionally attained."

CROW ISLAND SCHOOL

Europe experienced such social mayhem in the 1930s that avant-garde architects seemed desperate to design entirely new worlds. In America, the need for social change was less urgent, but still a strong idealistic streak underlay many major architectural projects. An important example of what might be termed "Euroamerican" modernism was Crow Island School, a design collaboration between Eliel Saarinen, his son Eero, and the Chicago firm of Perkins and Will. As a place that is lyrical in some ways and utterly practical in others, Crow Island School, in the North Shore suburb of Winnetka, was widely published and influenced school design for a generation.

The town's school system was extremely advanced in the late thirties and early forties. Its so-called Winnetka Plan loosened strict separations between disciplines and between grades, and its visionary superintendent at the time, Carleton Washburne, was determined to have a school that embodied his theory of education. He brought the Saarinens from the Cranbrook Academy of Art in Michigan, where they had moved after the Tribune Tower competition to teach and design the campus. Cranbrook—

Opposite: Crow Island School, 1112 Willow Road, Winnetka. Completed 1940, Eliel Saarinen and Eero Saarinen with Perkins and Will

A "beautiful, practical, homey, architectural embodiment of an educational philosophy" was the idea behind Crow Island School's modernism. Its simplified geometric shape was International in style, but its harmonies with the site and organic materials pay homage to the Prairie School. "The finish and settings must form harmonious background with honest child effort and creation," wrote a school administrator explaining Crow Island's design, which would influence school architecture for more than a generation.

Below right: The molded plywood chair was designed by the architects as inexpensive seating. It was also a vivid and curious form that could inspire the imagination.

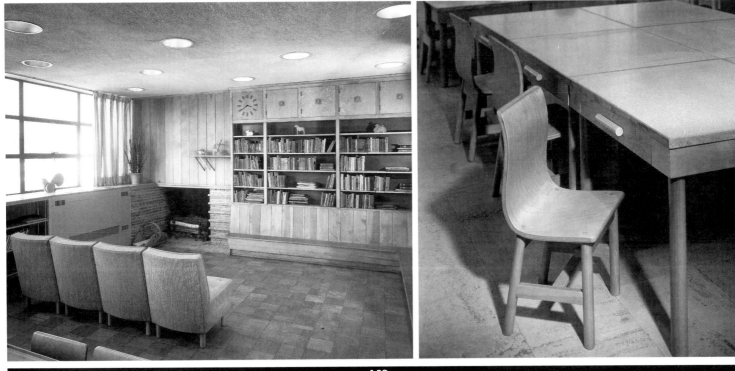

Left: Schweikher Residence, Schaumburg. Completed 1946, Paul Schweikher
Right: Rinaldo Residence, Downers Grove. Completed 1941, Paul Schweikher
Modern architect Paul Schweikher worked for David Adler early in his career and insisted that it was the master of eclectic mansions who taught him his unshakable sense of proportion. Schweikher later distinguished himself as a designer of modern suburban homes, of which his own was a masterpiece. Like the Prairie architects before him, he loved wood and brick. Like houses of the International style, the design was plain and unadorned. The result in this case was a country home of simplicity and extreme originality.

much in the spirit of other Saarinen work—was influenced by the formal modernism of Europe, but it retains a kind of warmth and organic connection to the site that is more akin to the traditions of Chicago architecture.

Like the designs of the Prairie School in decades past, Crow Island was built low to the ground and emphasized "local" materials like brick and wood. The school, which is still used, opens out onto its wooded site in many places, and other features reflect the ideas of organic architecture in more subtle ways. The school "should not seem complete and finished beyond any addition or adjustment to later demands," according to an *Architectural Forum* essay written by a Winnetka school administrator who was involved in the design. There should be a sense of craftwork, but since this was an elementary school it should not seem overly sophisticated. The simple brickwork of the place and the molded plywood furniture designed by the architects should "form a harmonious background with honest child effort and creation—not one which will make children's work seem crude." What was sought was a building that met not just the aesthetic needs of the site but also the psychological needs of the children inside.

MIES IN CHICAGO

Mies emerged as one of Europe's premier architects in the thirties, yet his greatest triumphs came in America and mostly in Chicago, where he came to head the School of Architecture at Armour (now Illinois) Institute of Technology. He left Germany with regret. He had tried to carve out a role for himself even as Nazi influence rose. He spent three years as director of the modern design school the Bauhaus, between 1930 and 1933 before it was closed. Mies himself was apolitical, and there is evidence that he tried to come to a personal truce with the Hitler government. But, ultimately, the Nazis tagged modern architecture "degenerate," and his prospects to work and succeed in his own country collapsed.

At the same time, there was something compelling about the United States. Compared to Germany at the time, it was aesthetically free, and it was a nation in the thrall of new and powerful technological powers. To put the contribution of Mies in the simplest terms, he was enchanted by the abundance of steel and its use in large buildings. It is no exaggeration to say that Mies developed the possibilities of steel in architecture more than anyone since William Le Baron Jenney. Beginning in Chicago, Mies's work opened the door to the proliferation of steel towers and the transformation of skylines around the world.

Mies's prior relationship with Chicago's existing traditions is an ambiguous and interesting issue. He had certainly studied the architecture of the Chicago School, as all European modernists had, and admired how well it suited its time. Mies once said, "We must learn to work with technology, using the materials of our time." Chicago was a natural place for him to call home. "All of Chicago," he continued, "was created in the spirit of the technological age." Yet it was by no means certain that Mies would settle in Chicago. In 1936 the first impetus to emigrate came from Joseph Hudnut, dean of the faculty of architecture at Harvard, who inquired about the possibility of his accepting a position at that school. Mies liked the idea and hoped to go to Boston, but he withdrew his name when he discovered that Harvard was vacillating on his appointment. Bringing such an extreme modernist to New England would have been interesting indeed—an experiment that may have been why Harvard balked.

Illinois Institute of Technology had no such misgivings. Its school of architecture was largely unformed and needed a leader to take charge. They found in Mies an architect who had strong ideas and a willingness to transmit them to students. And in Chicago,

Mies found a city with clear advantages. He was attracted above all by a history that long had been open to innovative architecture, certainly more than the Eastern cities that remained tied to the beaux-arts tradition. "Mies loved the power and clarity of Chicago buildings," says Myron Goldsmith, who worked for Mies between 1946 and 1953 and then went on to a distinguished career at Skidmore, Owings and Merrill. "Chicago gave Mies courage." On a more practical level, the steel mills near the city provided a relatively inexpensive source of the material that would distinguish his postwar buildings.

Mies's courage was justified by the equally courageous and forward-looking clients he found in Chicago. First in this group was Herbert Greenwald, a real estate developer who was twenty-nine years old when they met in 1946 and started their collaboration. The architectural history of Chicago, and that of other American cities, might be far different without Greenwald, who had left rabbinical studies to enter real estate. With an idea that he wanted to build large apartment towers, Greenwald decided that it would be an opportunity to form a relationship with an architect of international renown. Mies was on his list, as were Wright and Le Corbusier, and Greenwald was surprised to learn that the German was already in Chicago. Once the developer met the architect, Greenwald's philosophical training put him on equal footing with Mies's abstract "t'inking." Tragically, Greenwald died in a plane crash in 1958, but in their time together the Chicagoan enabled the esoteric Mies to build the first of his great glass apartment buildings and to become America's—which meant the world's—preeminent high-rise architect.

Glass towers, to be sure, were considered risky business in the late 1940s. Would people buy units with transparent walls dozens of stories above the street? In fact, they did. Homebuyers loved the light and willingly left their heavily draped, darker traditional interiors behind. Moreover, there was an unconventional grace to Mies's buildings. He was always a master of detail and proportion, and his earliest apartment buildings showed how a structure made entirely of steel and glass could please the eye in many ways. The twin towers at 860–880 North Lake Shore Drive, for example, became famous among architects for many reasons but among them was the technique of running structural I-beams up the outside of the buildings from the bottom to the top. These unadorned I-beams function indispensably as mullions for glass panels. Mies's great ingenuity made them decorative as well, giving the exterior a subtle touch of three-dimensionality that a sheer curtain wall would not otherwise have.

While Greenwald is remembered as a businessman who supported innovative architecture, Mies was an artist whose work corresponded with business objectives. Indeed, Mies was motivated in fundamental ways by economics. Flexible floor plans, for example, were a positive attribute of steel construction, a lesson that was first understood by the old Chicago School. So Mies designed the skeleton frame with a core for utilities down the center of the building, leaving the remainder of each floor largely open. Apartments could be divided into various sizes as the need arose. "To Mies, that was the sign of a good building, to maintain flexibility," says Joe Fujikawa, who worked on 860–880. "He always said that the ways we use buildings constantly change. The reason they tear buildings down is that they have outlived their usefulness."

Opposite: 860–880 North Lake Shore Drive. Completed 1952, Ludwig Mies van der Rohe
The residential skyscraper of glass and steel was one of Mies van der Rohe's major contributions to modern architecture, and 860–880 was his first important project of this kind. It seemed strange at the time that a building this simple could be elegant as well.

860–880 North Lake Shore Drive

Above: There was initial concern that people would resist skyscrapers with walls entirely of glass. On the contrary, the natural light and broad panoramas of Lake Michigan became enticing features for prospective residents.

Below: A study in an apartment in 860–880. Design by Powell/Kleinschmidt

Opposite, above: Mies van der Rohe's four towers on North Lake Shore Drive are shown here— 860–880 (left) and the Esplanade Apartments (right), 900–910 built in 1956.

Below left: Mies (with the help of the artists who worked for him) paid as much attention to the functional aspects of a dwelling as to the purely visual ones.

Below right: Mies designed the Brno chair for his Tugendhat House in the thirties, but even today it remains a likely addition to many modern interiors.

Crown Hall at Illinois Institute of Technology, 3360 South State Street. Completed 1956, Ludwig Mies van der Rohe

Above: Crown Hall became Mies's supreme experiment in universal space. Through the use of steel trusses above, the great hall is unencumbered by interior supports. By its of precise proportion, this building attains a repose and intimacy that makes it one of Chicago's most unexpectedly beautiful buildings.

Opposite, above: Mies's practical objective was to establish a *Bauhutte*, or place where students, artisans, and masters could work and interact. While large, the space is relatively easy to divide along the lines of the structural grid. Classes find comfort in small divisions of space, or larger groups can assemble, and the transparent walls implied by the architecture dissolve.

Opposite, below: Illinois Institute of Technology Chapel (Chapel of Saint Savior), 3200 South Michigan Avenue. Completed 1952, Ludwig Mies van der Rohe

It does not count among Chicago's most loved churches, but Mies's chapel demonstrates how a fine brick wall and a floor-to-ceiling curtain can inspire peace and contemplation. The architect was not religious in the conventional sense, but he believed that Christian philosophy could provide insight into modern problems, including those of design.

Mies's interest in flexibility in these apartment buildings evolved into a concept that became known as "universal space." This idea, once again, springs from the basic attributes of the architect's materials—that structural steel has the strength to construct spaces that are entirely flexible, without interior bearing walls or even supports to hinder changing needs. While Mies's European career focused on the creative geometric patterns of interconnecting rooms, in America it was the single, large, unencumbered interior that fascinated him. The sensation of universal space, moreover, could be expanded to the exterior and into infinity by the use of transparent glass walls. Mies obviously found this to be an interesting aesthetic exercise, and his finest examples of universal space can produce in visitors an almost supernatural calm. Yet again, Mies landed on an idea meant to be entirely practical as well.

Witness Crown Hall, which was built to house IIT's architecture and design schools. As Mies's biographer Franz Schulze explains, Crown Hall became the modern equivalent of the medieval *bauhütte*, a place large enough so that the master builder could work within view of apprentices and tradesmen at all times. For a school, the idea is admirable. In one universal space, students in different classes and at various levels can separate themselves for classwork, drafting, model building, and other activities. Yet there is interaction, cross-germination, and creativity born of being in the same place.

People at IIT disagree about whether or not the *bauhütte* idea works here, but the building itself perfectly suits the idea. Crown Hall's interior is entirely free of supporting members so division of space can be achieved by temporary partition. The space is large enough to allow groups to separate themselves for a lecture or work at tables. The most interesting feature of the building is one that is less visible—that division of the space can be achieved psychologically without walls or physical separations. Because of the architect's mastery of scale, the gridwork of the ceiling and the rhythm of the glass-paneled walls enable a group—even an individual—to feel an intimacy otherwise impossible in such a vast place. Space is shared, but the suggestion of "rooms" is implied. Implied space and transparent divisions become the crux of Mies's art. The irony of Crown Hall is that a building that appears to be the most minimal is actually the most complex. This minimalist approach that would seem eminently teachable actually becomes the most difficult, perhaps impossible, to transmit to students directly. Miesian architecture required not only an understanding of materials and function but also Mies's almost spiritual command of proportion.

THE TRIAL OF FARNSWORTH HOUSE

While Mies was the most artistic of architects, it is not surprising that he had his share of clashes with the real world. One such clash related to one of the masterpieces of his career, Farnsworth House, an exquisite glass and steel home that he designed for a friend, Dr. Edith Farnsworth. What began as a wonderful collaboration between architect and client ended with Mies being dismissed from the job before the interior was complete. Farnsworth also sued Mies, unsuccessfully, for a variety of sins, including cost overruns and even alleged incompetence.

No one knows precisely what happened in the Farnsworth case. There have been convincing suggestions of a romance between Farnsworth, a prominent Chicago physician, and Mies. When the relationship went sour, according to this version of the story, Mies was fired. It was fortunate that construction had been completed, with the exception of minor details and interior furnishings. Today the home is owned by a London real estate developer and architectural patron who has maintained the building in a state close to the intent of the architect. On the Fox River in tiny Plano,

Preceding page, above and opposite: Farnsworth House, Plano, Illinois. Completed 1951, Ludwig Mies van der Rohe

In this house, not far from the Fox River some fifty miles from Chicago, Mies used glass, steel, and travertine to create a whole new relationship between interior and exterior space. Farnsworth House has been tersely described as a glazed box floating on a steel frame. The point is that it really does seem to float, an effect that has everything to do with Mies's sense of proportion, his feel for materials, and his utter confidence in forms that had never been tried before. Though Mies contemplated a new line of furniture for Farnsworth House, it was never realized. The furniture shown here was disliked by Miesian purists.

Illinois, Farnsworth House is counted among the architectural landmarks of America. Its history also testifies to the fragility of the architectural process, at least one that was as refined as that practiced by Mies.

People who worked on Farnsworth House have said that Farnsworth, a highly intelligent and cultured woman, knew well what she was getting in hiring Mies van der Rohe. This could be an overstatement, given the fact that the house could be the apotheosis of universal space. But Myron Goldsmith, then a young Mies employee, insists that she was enthusiastic about the house from the beginning and often visited the site, bringing picnics on weekends. The house was immediately promising. As the steel frame went up, its classical rectangular proportions became evident. When the glass walls went up, there seemed to be no separation between inside and out. The architects working under Mies understood that the house might be the most intense expression of modern architecture ever built. They had reason to assume that the client was happy.

In the end, she was not. Conjecture about the reasons for this deteriorate into gossip and stories of jilted love. The outcome, however, was real. Mies did not finish the interior design of the place as he would have liked. Goldsmith says that Mies had several interesting ideas for furniture, such as chairs upholstered with untanned leather. Goldsmith points out, however, that Mies's office was not set up at this time to design furniture, so there is some doubt that he would have produced new furniture designs at all. What is clear is that the pieces Farnsworth eventually chose, a modern blondwood type from Italy, were by no means what the architect would have selected.

The issue between Mies and his client was not a matter of taste, however. Toward the end of the project, Goldsmith recalls that Farnsworth took him aside and said she was somewhat mystified that she and Mies had never discussed what his fee would be. Goldsmith, then a young apprentice architect, was surprised by this news but gave no reply. Later, in a five-week trial in a tiny rural courtroom where Farnsworth did battle with one of the world's most famous architects, unreasonable bills and alleged overruns commanded most of the judge's attention.

Issues in this unpleasant civil proceeding revolved around how much Mies said the place would cost, when he said it, and whether or not the price was guaranteed. Mies won the case, finally, based on the customary rules that govern the relationship between architect and client—which hold that architects can provide only estimates. But one small episode during this case is telling. It was recounted in an interview years later by architect Paul Schweikher, who was an expert witness on behalf of Mies. Schweikher said that just before the trial Mies told him that he found a "notation" written after an early meeting with the client. It was a paper that stated, apparently before construction began, that projected costs for the house were only an estimate.

Schweikher was careful not to vouch for the utter truth of the story. Nor was this "notation" remembered as a critical piece of evidence in the verdict. But there is something symbolic about this tale. Mies said that the document had been used as a bookmark and had turned up between the pages of a book by Friedrich Nietzsche. One of Mies's favorite philosophers, Nietzsche believed in the "superman," and that creativity and passion would free humanity from the bonds of everyday life. Like Mies, he might have scorned the distractions of patrons and clients. In the real world, however, keeping them calm and happy was necessary to the kind of life that both the architect and the philosopher coveted.

Opposite: Farnsworth House
Utilitarian touches in the kitchen do not spoil the imposing elegance inside and out.

In the 1960s and 1970s, as the firm of Skidmore, Owings and Merrill pushed the technical limits of skyscrapers, it was easy to wonder if architecture was any longer of this world. In previous generations, Louis Sullivan claimed kinship with Walt Whitman. Mies invoked Saint Thomas Aquinas. Skidmore, Owings and Merrill, on the other hand, was an organization, not a person, and skyscrapers such as Sears Tower were known more for engineering than for art.

But Skidmore, Owings and Merrill, SOM to its friends, was a creature of its time, and its direction was cast by individuals who were as passionate in their own way as their more romantic predecessors. First among them was Louis Skidmore, who began his career as a young architect in Chicago during the depression. It was a bad time for architects, and Skidmore was lucky enough to be made chief designer of the 1933 Century of Progress. The organizers of this event, Chicago's second great world's fair, were determined to make it a technological wonder and not a mere trade show, and Skidmore was the person responsible for enforcing the architectural standards. He approved designs that met the futuristic theme—Kecks' House of Tomorrow among them—and turned down others that fell short. Nor was the rakish young architect cowed by the rich and powerful: among his rejects was a forty-five-foot pyramid of vinegar bottles, the pavilion of H. J. Heinz Company. John Heinz himself stormed, "Who is this wax-mustache bozo in the raccoon coat and earmuffs who turned down my display?" But Skidmore held his ground, which earned him more admiration than enmity. He went on to build a firm with major offices in Chicago, New York, and San Francisco that would change the look of corporate America.

Skidmore was his era's equivalent of Daniel Burnham. Both were central figures in world's fairs; both excelled more at salesmanship and organization than design. Just as inspired architecture sometimes eluded D. H. Burnham and Company, the buildings of SOM often were noted for their size and not their ability to stir souls. But like Burnham, SOM designed several buildings that would become Chicago icons.

INLAND'S STAINLESS IMAGE

The story of SOM's enormous influence on Chicago architecture begins with the Inland Steel Building, which was completed in 1958. It was only the second major new building in downtown Chicago since the depression. As though it represented much pent-up creativity, Inland Steel remains one of the landmark structures of its era. In the constant effort of high-rise architects to master gravity, this nineteen-story tower took several additional steps forward. Supported by steel columns around the perimeter, the building contains clear-span space on each of its floors—a core with elevators and stairwells is located to the side. The Inland Steel Building essentially represents

Opposite: Inland Steel Building, 30 West Monroe Street. Completed 1957, Skidmore, Owings and Merrill

Only the second major downtown building since the depression, the nineteen-story Inland Steel headquarters had a major influence on the design of other corporate buildings. Its exterior cast an indisputably modern image for the company. Its interior featured the most flexible floor plan possible. Specially designed furniture enhanced the openness of the offices and also utilized products sold by the client itself. Today the Inland Steel Building remains eminently practical, aesthetically unified, and ever fresh to the eye.

Inland Steel Building
Steel mesh was among the Inland-made industrial materials that were fashioned into elegant furniture for the executive offices in the Inland Steel Building.
Opposite, above: Davis Allen's so-called tin desk, Mies's Barcelona chair, and a Willem DeKooning painting combine in a still-modern design in the Inland Steel offices.
Opposite, below: The clear-span space of Inland Steel's interior gave designers total freedom to divide offices with complete flexibility using glass partitions.

universal space built high. It was also the most appropriate of structures for its particular client, as the stainless steel used in its construction was an important product sold by the company that would occupy it.

Stainless steel not only graces the exterior of Inland Steel but is used extensively inside as well. It was, in fact, the interiors that drew the most attention when the building was completed, and the story behind this aspect of Inland Steel testifies, once again, to the importance of clients in the design process. They were Leigh Block, the chairman of the company, and Mary Block, his wife, who had inspired plans for a glass and steel corporate headquarters—with little precedent except New York's Lever House, also by SOM. By 1956 structural design for the Inland building had been settled, but the interior had not, when the Blocks left for a vacation that would take them to Istanbul. Quite naturally, Louis Skidmore asked one of his architects working on another SOM project, the Istanbul Hilton, to look in on his wealthy clients when they arrived. That man was Davis Allen, who took the Blocks on a whirlwind tour of the city—dining with the British ambassador and yachting on the Bosphorus. He also invited them for a look at his own work on the interior of the Hilton. This design was later described by partner Nathaniel Owings as "a salubrious blend of strong Turkish architectural motifs and American plumbing and heating." In fact, Allen had done what would become increasingly important in modern architecture. He gave otherwise plain modernist buildings distinct and memorable touches. The Blocks wanted Allen to apply his talents to their building in Chicago.

When he arrived in Chicago, Allen had several luxuries to work with in the Inland Steel Building. One was the clear-span space on each floor, entirely free of interior columns. The other was the Blocks' interest in purchasing large-scale modern art for their headquarters, and this would include works by Alexander Calder, Willem de Kooning, Harry Bertoia, and Seymour Lipton. Pieces such as these, as well as the handsome exterior of the building, provided considerable inspiration for Allen, who designed an elegant but thoroughly modern environment for the company. "They didn't

want any of that pseudo-Chippendale baloney," Allen said of the Blocks. Instead he chose Mies van der Rohe and Georg Jensen furniture and also worked with different manufacturers to create office suites that were as original as the building itself.

It was natural for steel to become the principal expression of the interior as it was on the exterior. For executive offices, Allen designed lounge chairs made of industrial-grade steel mesh. The boardroom table, known as "the surfboard," was accompanied by leather-upholstered chairs on slender, slightly splayed steel legs. Allen also designed the so-called "tin desk" for the Inland offices, and its simple, economical design was quickly adopted by the furniture company that manufactured it, Steelcase, as one of its trademark products. Inland's was one of the first interiors to be integrated so completely with modernist architecture on such a large scale. "What was true outside became true inside," remarked Allen. What was a handsome piece of architecture inside and out also became a convincing blend of technology and corporate image making. Other corporations, including Chase Manhattan Bank in New York City, would follow with SOM designing equally distinctive urban monuments for them.

JOHN HANCOCK AND THE EFFECTS OF SCALE

The success of SOM was unprecedented in the two decades that followed as many corporate headquarters, apartment buildings, college campuses, and other major works were commissioned. As with most enterprises that achieve this level of success, a modicum of luck was involved. In SOM's case it was that the firm entered its heyday during one of the largest economic expansions in history. As the firm reached maturity, its commissions grew fantastically both in number and in size. During the sixties and seventies, the large-scale vision of the firm corresponded perfectly with that of many

John Hancock Center, North Michigan Avenue between Chestnut and Delaware streets. Completed 1968, Skidmore, Owings and Merrill

Opposite: Its diagonal trusses were an engineering triumph when John Hancock was built. John Hancock was an unexpected artistic success as well. Its famous tapered profile actually began as a practical solution for the architects, providing a large floor plate for offices on lower floors and a smaller one for apartments above.

Below: The apartment lobby is on the forty-fourth floor of the John Hancock Center.

John Hancock Center
Above: Diagonal trusses became a desirable design feature in the John Hancock Center apartments.
Below: A model apartment in John Hancock, 1966.

Opposite: Sears Tower, bounded by Wacker Drive, Jackson Boulevard, Franklin Street, and Adams Street. Completed 1974, Skidmore, Owings and Merrill
The world's tallest building demonstrates that seemingly stark modernism can be elegant. While the engineering feat of Sears Tower was in its steel-tube construction—the building is a cluster of nine self-contained vertical sections—it also reflects the artistic lessons of Art Deco skyscrapers built in the twenties. Soaring piers and graceful setbacks are combined to accommodate mechanical systems, maximize natural light, and create an imposing image from miles and miles away.

clients. In this period SOM counted the tallest and fourth tallest buildings in the world, Chicago's Sears Tower and John Hancock Center among their achievements. Bruce Graham was credited as chief architect on these projects, but the buildings were successful mainly because SOM was an organization of many individuals who could solve the multitude of problems inherent in such projects. Teamwork was critical in buildings as formidable as Hancock, completed in 1968, and Sears, completed in 1974. Both were engineered as giant steel tubes, conceptually simple but taller and with much larger spans than other office buildings that were then going up.

Among the important contributors at SOM at this time was architect-engineer Myron Goldsmith, whose experience included working for Mies in the forties and fifties and later with Pier Luigi Nervi, an innovator of curvilinear modernist forms in postwar Italy. Goldsmith's master's thesis at IIT in 1953, entitled "The Effects of Scale," examined the idea that structures of different size have different ideal forms. He analyzed Gothic cathedrals, the Monadnock Building, nineteenth-century railroad sheds, and Mies's steel and glass designs—all as calculated solutions to specific problems of scale. As Goldsmith's career progressed, he dedicated himself to helping design forms for buildings that grew increasingly larger, with spans that were increasingly longer. At SOM he worked closely with engineer Fazlur Khan and Graham. Together they ushered in an era of skyscrapers of unprecedented size.

Their achievements were not only feats of engineering but also harmonious architecture. Among the firm's projects, the John Hancock Center has become one of Chicago's most admired skyscrapers partly because of its success as a mixed-use structure on Michigan Avenue, Chicago's most fashionable boulevard. More important, perhaps, has been the building's clear and distinct image against the sky. Its diagonal trusses—a postulation in Goldsmith's master's thesis years before—saved the developers millions of dollars in the cost of steel needed to support such a building. The tapering of the skyscraper was important so that the highest stories with residential apartments would be smaller and more filled with natural light than the office floors below. With such practicalities considered, the tower points toward the clouds with seeming effortlessness and with beauty akin to the work of Louis Sullivan.

It only seems effortless, of course. Beyond the technical skill required to design and build Hancock, marketing savvy was necessary to justify such a massive building. The architects played a prominent role in this process as well. In 1967, for example, when only the frame of the skyscraper was up, SOM built a small temporary building nearby with mock-ups of one-, two-, and three-bedroom apartments. The interiors featured contemporary design, naturally, but included a blend of period furniture as well. The objective was to prove that antiques could be used in a modern building, even one with a large diagonal truss across some windows. For that reason, the models included a facsimile of a truss, and this surprising feature itself became a selling point for prospective buyers.

MCCORMICK PLACE

Skidmore, Owings and Merrill was successful because of its rapport with good clients. Not all successful buildings, however, have been so blessed. An example was the second McCormick Place, a project that overcame politics and indecision of near-catastrophic proportions and still succeeded at producing a grand and memorable building. The project began in 1967, the day after the original McCormick Place burned to the ground. No sooner had the embers died than Mayor Richard J. Daley called the firm of C. F. Murphy Associates to start planning a new one. This choice of

McCormick Place, 22nd Street and Lake Michigan. Completed 1971, C. F. Murphy and Associates

Above and following page, above: McCormick Place went through several design revisions before the simplest and most Miesian of schemes was agreed upon. It was designed by Gene Summers, a former protégé of Mies, and it succeeds as a masterwork of proportion on Chicago's lakefront.

Following page, below: The overhangs in McCormick Place are seventy feet wide all around, adding to the sense of indoor-outdoor space

firms was predictable. C. F. Murphy was considered "palace architect" to the adminis-tration of the first Mayor Daley, and most important public work was going their way.

The following day, a partner from the Murphy office called a young architect, Gene Summers, to convince him to join the firm and undertake the design of the new McCormick Place. It was a tempting proposal for Summers, who was then in his thirties. The building's lakefront site was stupendous. It was an opportunity for interior space on an unprecedented scale. But Summers had recently left the office of Mies van der Rohe to go off on his own, and he seemed determined to build his practice. He listened to Murphy's offer over lunch at the Arts Club. At the end he said he would consider it only under conditions that he himself regarded as outrageous. Murphy would have to make him a 10-percent partner of the firm. He must also be given the position of director of design over the entire firm, not just the McCormick Place project. Summers left the Arts Club that afternoon assuming the matter was ended, but the next day Charles Murphy himself called to finalize a deal. So began an architectural marriage that was, at least initially, mismatched and troubled.

The history of C. F. Murphy Associates goes back to 1911, when Charles F. Murphy, a nonarchitect from Chicago's South Side, was hired as a typist at D. H. Burnham and Company. Burnham died a year later, and Murphy joined its successor firm of Graham, Anderson, Probst and White, becoming personal assistant to Ernest R. Graham. When Graham died in 1936, Murphy fell out with the heirs of the firm and went off to start a new one, initially called Shaw, Naess and Murphy (later Naess and Murphy). This firm grew slowly until 1955, when it designed the Prudential Building. This was the first major building in downtown Chicago since the depression, and for more than a decade it was the city's tallest. The firm's fortunes soared a few years later with its design for Chicago's Central District Water Filtration Plant. This project, set beside Navy Pier, overcame much political resistance by virtue of an attractive modern design for which Mayor Daley was eternally grateful. A long string of public commissions followed—many large though few architecturally significant—including O'Hare Airport in 1963.

Summers, for his part, was more artist than political insider. One of his first jobs in architecture had been to work on the interior core of Mies's Farnsworth House. He later became a lead designer and supervisor on several important commissions in the Mies van der Rohe office, including the National Gallery in Berlin. When Summers went off to practice on his own, his idea was to have a small office operating much like that of Mies, who was a deliberate thinker and never hurried to solve creative problems. Perhaps hoping to cultivate such a setting for the McCormick Place commission, Summers went to Mies and invited him to collaborate, especially since the older man had designed an unbuilt convention hall for Chicago some years before. "Not if it was the Parthenon on the Acropolis," Mies replied. He was near the end of his career. He also knew Chicago politics. Summers was on his own.

Summers recalls that the design of McCormick Place seemed star-crossed from the start. Problems began with the general manager of the city's convention authority, who insisted that the new building be a multistory structure. The reasons for this eluded almost everyone involved in the project, but Summers obeyed. The result was that his first scheme for the building was a total flop, which embarrassed Summers, but he gamely went back to the drawing board. His second scheme was more what people expected from a modernist of Summers's stature. It was a large universal space beneath a bridgelike structure with suspension cables overhead. Drawings of this scheme show a handsome design, and it won considerable praise in the convention and tourism industry and among architects. Unfortunately, it was unloved by Henry Crown, a powerful Chicago industrialist and relative of Arie Crown, for whom the theater in old McCormick Place was named. In Summers's new scheme, the theater was down-sized and placed underground. Summers was sent back to try once again.

Depressed and by now under considerable time constraints, Summers was some-thing less original in his third try—a giant pavilion with proportions that resembled previous buildings by Mies. The difference was that this structure had grown to mammoth size—made structurally possible with an innovative truss system. The invention of this truss system has a significant history: it was worked out by Summers's young associate on the project, a former IIT student named Helmut Jahn, and its direct antecedent was a scheme for a large hall by an architectural student named Paul Zorr, who conceived such a structure, never built, as his master's thesis at IIT in 1967.

Among the charms of McCormick Place are its siting, neatly tucked between Lake Shore Drive and Lake Michigan. Seventy-foot overhangs and expansive glass walls create an indoor-outdoor feeling, enhanced by an open sight line from the entrance through the building and out over Lake Michigan. In the end, Miesian architecture needs no further justification than McCormick Place. It solved the problem of ample space for large conventions. It also satisfied the political arbiters who originally seemed destined to ruin chances for an inspired design.

BERTRAND GOLDBERG:
ON CORNCOBS AND CONCRETE

In the fifties and sixties, the glass and steel rectangles of the International style were preeminent, and few alternatives were being considered by architects in Chicago. One exception was Bertrand Goldberg, a native Chicagoan who had studied at the German Bauhaus for about a year during the short period that Mies headed the school. Goldberg returned to America in 1933 just before the Bauhaus, which was considered dangerously radical by the Nazis, was closed. He was deeply influenced by what he learned in Europe but was just as determined to go his own way. In Chicago, Goldberg witnessed the Century of Progress and its architecture, which was modern, stream-lined, and generally more decorative than the International style. Goldberg gradually renounced the cold intellectualism, even somberness, that often characterized the Miesians and developed an approach that became very much his own.

Early in his career, Goldberg worked in the office of Keck and Keck and grew fond of prefabrication. He designed the prototype for a chain of ice cream shops called the North Pole in 1938. This design, supported by cables from a central post, prefigured a similar and more famous design, Buckminster Fuller's Dymaxion House, built two years later. If mainstream architecture in this era tended toward plainness and uniformity, Goldberg rebelled by being unpredictable. Unpredictable would also describe Ma-rina City when it was built in 1961. It remains one of Chicago's most distinctive buildings—Goldberg himself has called it, perhaps hyperbolically, the most photo-graphed building in the world.

Opposite, above: Prefabricated Bathroom, 1946, Bertrand Goldberg
Goldberg had a philosophical break with Mies van der Rohe and his followers shortly after his return from studies at the Bauhaus. Goldberg worked for a time with the Kecks and developed a taste for prefabrication. Concentrating on the practical needs of people, his attention turned, quite naturally, toward the bath.

Opposite, below: North Pole Ice Cream Parlor, River Forest. Completed 1938, Bertrand Goldberg
An early Goldberg commission was for this prototype for a chain of ice cream stores. A central column and cable supports—drawn from techniques used a few years before at the Century of Progress—was part of Goldberg's search for a style that could be both economical and pleasant.

The curvaceous lines of the two towers of Marina City have been likened to the Spanish church architecture of Antonio Gaudi. Other descriptions compare them to two giant corncobs, and whether or not Goldberg had this agricultural motif in mind beforehand, he approved of the analogy. He said that the loss of grain elevators in downtown Chicago, probably around the turn of the century, marked the end of the river as a working thoroughfare, and that was when "the confusion of the American city began."

Goldberg believes that his erstwhile mentor, Mies, cared mainly about theoretically perfect, impersonal buildings that had little to do with social forces all around. Goldberg, in contrast, says that he thinks constantly about the fate of cities. The design for Marina City, in fact, began in the late fifties as a response to the flight of middle-class families to the suburbs, amidst predictions that cities as places to live were doomed. The client of this project was significant—William McFetridge, head of the union of elevator operators and building janitors, whose membership was bound to suffer as economic vitality left downtown Chicago. McFetridge and Goldberg's interest was to create a new center of life in the city, which meant overcoming a variety of serious forces against them. Zoning laws, for example, then prohibited an apartment/retail/recreation/office complex. In an environment that seemed increasingly unfriendly, the architect's challenge was to regain a sense of neighborhood.

Marina City, on the Chicago River between State and Dearborn streets. Completed 1961, Bertrand Goldberg

At a time of exodus from the central city, Goldberg designed a complex that would reinstill a sense of neighborhood downtown. Apartments, offices, shops, and other amenities were built into twin towers that remain among Chicago's most distinctive buildings. Though Goldberg was a student of Mies in the thirties, he rejected the master's approach to architecture as too formal and impersonal. Concrete construction replaced Mies's expensive steel frames, and round forms replaced rectilinear ones. While Goldberg's relentless practicality is typically American, his staunch individualism foreshadowed the rise of postmodernism.

Below: The floor plan for Marina City demonstrated that modernism need not be boxed.

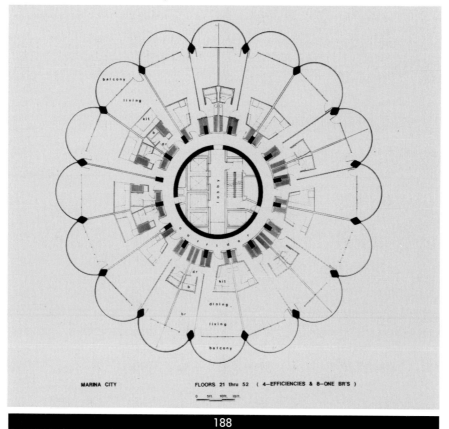

MARINA CITY   FLOORS 21 thru 52   (4—EFFICIENCIES & 8—ONE BR'S)

While Mies sometimes admitted that people would "learn" to live in his buildings, his former student Goldberg found this idea distasteful. "I am not trying to modify society through architecture," he once said. "I am trying to reflect society through architecture." In his search for ways to achieve that goal, he found concrete, not steel, a more appropriate material. (Marina City was the tallest concrete building in the world when it was built.) Concrete was cheaper and more suitable in a project designed not just for wealthy cliff dwellers but for a true middle class. Concrete had the additional advantage of plasticity in constructing the round forms Goldberg preferred. "I was revolting against a century of static space, against the straight line, against the idea of a man made in the image of a machine," he said. Goldberg continues to insist that the main reason for boxlike architecture in cities today is economic. Grids, not curves, are the easiest way for developers to calculate return on investment.

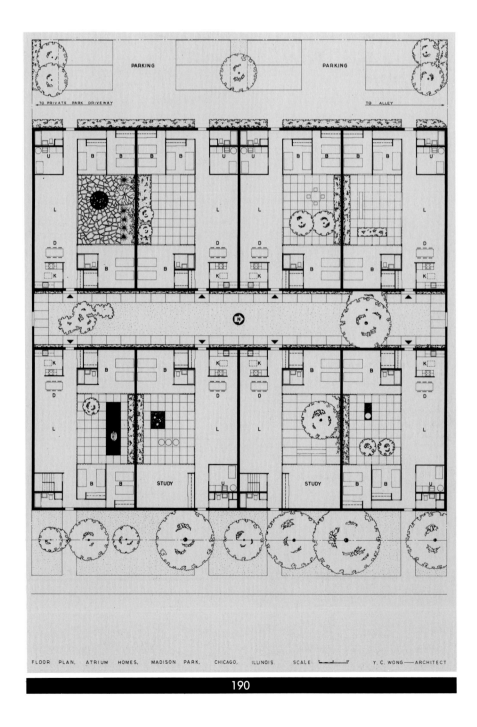

FLOOR PLAN, ATRIUM HOMES, MADISON PARK, CHICAGO, ILLINOIS. SCALE ⊢━━━┤' Y. C. WONG—ARCHITECT

Atrium Homes, 1370 East Madison Park. Completed 1961, Y. C. Wong

Wong was a student and later an employee of Mies. In his Atrium Houses in Chicago's Hyde Park neighborhood, the concept of enclosed courtyards provide a sense of freedom often absent in traditional houses of the same size. The innovation of Wong's design lies in his ability to achieve open space, ample light, and economy in urban homes. Like the architecture of Mies, Wong's surfaces are plain but never without the interest of studied textures and geometric form.

Opposite: The floor plan of Atrium Homes shows a deceptively open use of space.

A. J. Speyer Apartment, Chicago. Completed 1963, A. J. Speyer

Above: No one demonstrated the timelessness of good design like the late James Speyer, an architect and long-time curator of twentieth-century art at the Art Institute of Chicago. He was a close friend of Mies, and this view of Speyer's apartment shows that the influence was deeply felt. Yet Speyer used art and antiques more lavishly than Mies himself ever did. The eighteenth-century icons are from Greece. The rugs are kilims. The chairs are Mies van der Rohe.

Below: The Speyer dining room had a Le Corbusier table and MR chairs by Mies. The painting is entitled *Real Love and Hard Work*, 1966, by Chicago imagist artist Peter Saul.

Another highly independent architect of the fifties and sixties was Edward Dart, who like Goldberg diverged from the predictable modernism of his time. Until late in his career, Dart concentrated on human-scale buildings, which included residences and churches with interiors of striking originality. Later he applied his architecture with its concentration on flowing space to larger commercial structures, including the urban shopping mall Water Tower Place.

Dart was a native New Orleanian who went to Yale University, graduating in 1949. While at Yale he studied under a number of distinguished modern architects who were teaching there on a rotating basis, Louis Kahn and Eero Saarinen among them. Another of his college teachers was Paul Schweikher, a former draftsman for David Adler and later a distinguished designer of suburban homes. After graduation, Dart went to work for Schweikher in his suburban Chicago studio. The young man was attracted to Schweikher's work, which combined the minimalism of the International style with a thoroughly midwestern feel for modest materials like unpainted wood and brick. Dart was attracted even more by the architectural setting of Chicago at large, where he believed progressive architecture was accepted as it was nowhere else. "He did not want to build Cape Cod houses which seemed to be all the fashion in the East," said Dart's sister, Susan McCutcheon, in her biography of Dart. After two years with Schweikher, Dart went off on his own and quickly found willing clients for his contemporary style. Dart loved such modest finishes as exposed beams and common brick, and he assembled them in ways that achieved unique and pleasing effects in space and light. By 1955 his work was regarded as prominent enough to be part of an architectural tour organized by Lake Forest College, which also included houses by Wright, the Kecks, and other architects who then seemed radical on the usually sedate North Shore.

It was in usually staid churches that Dart's original approach to interior space came across most vividly. Churches have always represented enviable opportunities for architects; in the sixties they were particularly challenging as the very relevance of religion was being questioned throughout society. In the Catholic church, which was undergoing changes inspired by Vatican II, a reassessment of religion's role led to an architecture that was more down-to-earth than imposing. Some church officials described the process as self-examination, a turning inward. In this sense, the problem was custom-made for architects who concentrated on interior space, and Edward Dart was near the top of this list.

Among Dart's many churches in the Chicago area, First Saint Paul's Evangelical Lutheran, built in the midst of the major urban renewal of Sandburg Village, is one of his best known. The brick steepleless church appears so simple that passersby don't always know it is a church. Yet it satisfied a variety of complex needs that were important to the pastor who was the client. It should blend, not clash, with the modern neighborhood. Yet it should suit traditional parishioners of the church, the oldest Lutheran congregation in Chicago. No ready antecedents presented themselves. But it was typical of Dart that he should think first of the space, then of the walls to enclose it. When First Saint Paul's was finished in 1970, it was not surprising that the structure should look modern. What was curious was that the pastor later said that the largely unadorned brick interior became a place for "a much more ancient type of worship."

Inside, the ellipse at the end of the nave is indeed cavelike. It implies a chancel or sanctuary more than it separates one space from another, contributing to the idea that the division between altar and congregation is not strict but rather gradual. The

interior is plain but has a number of elegant features: a brick baffle that decorates but also absorbs echoes, and clerestory windows with light streaming in on the altar. Granite lectern and baptismal font are bold forms where the eye can easily rest. Dart used these pieces as he used antiques in residential designs—to provide moments of respite in a deceptively complex series of spaces.

Residences, churches, and other buildings of a human scale kept Dart busy through most of his career. Then in 1965 he joined the large commercial firm of Loebl, Schlossman and Bennett. There he embarked on a commission that was at once the most impressive and most frustrating of his life. Water Tower Place would be a huge mixed-use project anchored by a great vertical indoor shopping center. Water Tower Place, once again, demonstrated Dart's skill in designing interiors—here on a grand, urban scale. The mall constitutes a sequence of interconnected spaces moving from the street, up escalators, and into an open, balconied atrium. It was much appreciated when completed in 1974. Less applauded, at least initially, was the exterior, which many critics attacked as hopelessly plain and "a shapeless montage." But as good buildings do, this one has aged well. Its simplicity and proportions have retained a

Opposite and above: First Saint Paul's Evangelical Lutheran Church, 1301 North LaSalle Street. Completed 1970, Edward Dart

Except for the crosses, the exterior of First Saint Paul's bears little resemblance to a conventional church, but inside it houses what its pastor called an "ancient type of worship." Dart's mastery of space is manifest in the way he conceived form, utilized building materials, and even handled acoustics with a textured brick "baffle" in the sanctuary. While First Saint Paul's is innovative and almost radical in design, it remains stately and harmonious among townhouses and high-rise apartments in a neighborhood that was one of Chicago's largest urban renewal districts in the sixties.

fresh look admired on North Michigan Avenue, where later buildings with more decoration look dated by comparison. Inside, the commercial space of Water Tower is the least pretentious—and most profitable—of a number of other retail centers in the area.

The tragedy of Water Tower Place was that the building could have been integrated even more with the architectural fabric of Chicago. But instead of Dart's choice of granite for the building, the developers insisted on a shiny white marble, which inspired one critic to call it "men's room modern." People who knew Dart at the time say that the decision was a travesty for the architect, but he was powerless in the face of clients who were paying $160 million for the building. "He was caught in the big business trap," said Ed Straka, an associate of Dart's from the small-firm days. "His latest work was devoid of human touch," which is a harsh but understandable criticism. Dart's sister believes that Water Tower Place highlighted for him the error in moving to a large firm, and that it contributed to his sudden death in 1975, which was caused by a brain embolism at the age of fifty-three.

Water Tower Place, Michigan Avenue and Chestnut Street. Completed 1974, Loebl, Schlossman, Bennett and Dart

Unloved when it was built, Water Tower Place has "aged well" and today seems more contemporary than many of its recent neighbors. It testifies to Dart's skill at devising a series of dramatic and interesting spaces and enclosing them in a simple, well-proportioned shell. The shiny marble of the exterior was not Dart's choice; he preferred a less showy stone more in keeping with Chicago's democratic character. But the developers prevailed in this issue, which was the most discouraging battle of the architect's life. In most high-rise buildings, moving from one level to another is a mundane if not irritating interlude. In Water Tower, it is an experience of moving through space. Between entryway and "mall" is a long and luxurious escalator. Water Tower's elevators were among the first to make ascension into true spectacle.

Haid Residence, Evanston. Completed 1968, David Haid

David Haid was a student and employee of Mies's in the fifties and later planned courtyard homes as urban redevelopment projects. Haid's work calls to mind something Mies once said: "Building has obviously less to do with the invention of new forms than with the organization in a construction of the clearly defined relationship between things." Haid's own one-story home, thoroughly International in style, sits comfortably in a neighborhood of grand Queen Annes.

Opposite: Space flows from room to room and into the exterior courtyard of the Haid residence. The lot is small and the street relatively busy, but the house achieves a sure sense of spaciousness and privacy.

Haid Residense

Above: A bedroom in the Haid residence.

Opposite: As in the work of Mies, the materials are rich and the proportions are precise, as evident in the Haid living room.

As architecture moved from modern to postmodern, there was logic and even justice in the fact that Chicago embraced the most unpredictable and controversial architect of the time, Helmut Jahn. Chicago, after all, had given rise to the glass towers of Mies van der Rohe and by association bore guilt for a generation of callow Miesian imitators. It was inevitable that hostility toward modernism would grow. It was also inevitable that when the architectural pendulum did swing back, it did so most dramatically in Chicago, and especially with Jahn, whose mission was to prove that architecture was not limited by the minimalism of the International style. Modern technology, rather, made any form, even whimsical ones, possible. Jahn's rise corresponded with the fashion for postmodernism, a widespread style that delighted in nothing more than making historical forms look modern and modern forms look historical. Today it is difficult to classify Jahn as a postmodernist, a mostly discredited movement that does not square with Jahn's still soaring career. Yet his fascination with architectural history, from classicism to Art Deco, suggests that he shares the postmodern impatience with plain, interchangeable skyscrapers.

Audacious does describe Jahn, however, as he redefines skylines—or at least sections of them—with a single stroke of what some call his "Classics Comics" architecture. Helmut Jahn has become an international star with projects going well beyond Chicago. He has had many commissions in Germany, and he has designed an airport of unimaginably vast dimensions for Jeddah, Saudi Arabia. Appropriately enough, he also has been doing studies for Disneyland. His buildings are often otherworldly. Early in his career he earned the nickname "Flash Gordon."

It is fair to ask, however, if Jahn sometimes pushes the limits of convention too far, and if he did so in the State of Illinois Center, which was dedicated in 1985. Sometimes called "Starship Chicago," the building is not widely loved by Chicagoans. What disturbs local people about this building (which is heartily admired by many European critics) is not that it is radical or even jarring—Chicago has never suppressed experiments in design. Rather, Jahn's supremely odd building speaks an architectural language that many people, despite their best efforts, simply do not comprehend. This public structure became a political issue in 1986 when Governor James Thompson, who commissioned it, faced reelection. Thompson won despite a barrage of criticism over the building, its design, and its immense cost overruns.

The broad outline of the State of Illinois Center appears to be inspired by a classical ellipse—a dome, perhaps, which has been brought down to the ground. It is an interesting idea for a government building, even a noble one, except in this case there is a disconcerting sensation that the building leans. If Jahn's intention was to suggest that the structure defies gravity (which might correspond to a series of decorative columns in front that are unconnected to the building), one hopes that in time the idea will be understood and accepted. What seems unacceptable, even irritating, is that the color scheme of light blue and salmon resembles a discount department store more than a government center.

Nevertheless, the State of Illinois building has impressive elements. Its entrance and

Opposite and following pages: Lake Point Tower, Grand Avenue at Lake Shore Drive. Completed 1968, Schipporeit-Heinrich Associates

One of Chicago's most desirable high-rise residences, it typifies architecture from the inside out. Lake Point Tower is supported by a central column that leaves interior space free to be divided and assembled at will. Its curvaceous three-leaf floor plate assures the best possible views for all rooms within. Originally a rental building, it was later converted into condominiums, a great success because of the building's beauty as well as the utter flexibility in the subdivision of each floor.

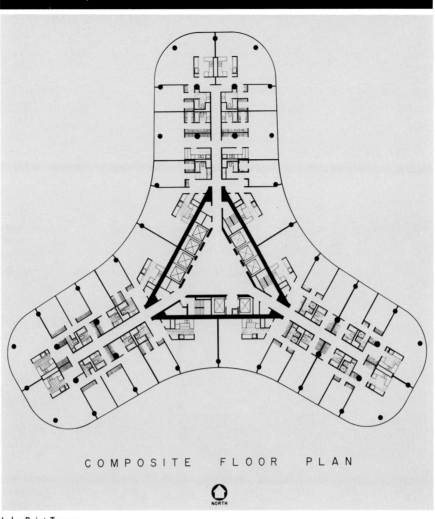

COMPOSITE FLOOR PLAN

NORTH

Lake Point Tower
Structurally, it applied lessons that were tried and tested, but the floor plan of Lake Point Tower provides residents inside with breathtaking views of Lake Michigan and the city.

---

small plaza are angled toward a busy intersection; across this is the Daley Center courts building and its own larger plaza. These connected outdoor spaces relieve congestion of the otherwise crowded Loop and also provide a place for public activity—for music, festivals, and public demonstrations. Moreover, the exterior space outside the State of Illinois Center flows smoothly to the indoor atrium of the seventeen-story structure. To his credit, Jahn acceded to Ruskin's Lamp of Sacrifice. The interior is magnificent and costly.

Despite the State of Illinois Center, Helmut Jahn has proven himself to be an architect with roots in Chicago's architectural tradition. He arrived in Chicago from West Germany at the age of twenty-five, lured by the legacy of Mies van der Rohe. He studied briefly at IIT with Myron Goldsmith and Fazlur Khan. In 1967 he joined Gene Summers at C. F. Murphy Associates as a design associate on McCormick Place. When Summers left C. F. Murphy in 1973, Jahn replaced him as director of design, and his rise through the firm was meteoric. He understood the general disenchantment with glass-box modernism. He himself complained that an architect should be more than "the mere translator of economical, social, and technical forces." He gave his imagination a freer reign and struck a chord with many developers at the time. So

powerful was Jahn's role as both designer and salesman that he was made president of C. F. Murphy in 1982. The following year he bought out the Murphy family to assume full control.

Jahn's triumph was to steer the firm around a critical corner, from conservative modernism to the changing tastes of corporations and developers. One of Jahn's first designs in this vein was Chicago's Xerox Centre, built in 1980. Xerox was understated, but it differed from post-Miesian plainness and responded to its site in ways that were uncommon at the time. The sleek white skyscraper defers graciously to its next-door neighbor, the old Marquette Building by Holabird and Roche, by being set back a few feet on Dearborn Street. On the other side of the tower, Jahn emphasizes the intersection of Dearborn and Monroe streets with a rounded corner, a gesture that recalls Sullivan's Carson Pirie Scott building only two blocks away. Xerox was original but not outlandish.

More large commissions followed, and as Jahn's buildings became more sculptural

Above and opposite: State of Illinois Center; Randolph, LaSalle, Lake, and Clark streets. Completed 1984, Murphy/Jahn

This has been one of the most controversial buildings in Chicago's history. Conceptually, it is interesting, but its individualism has yet to capture the hearts of Chicagoans. Finding drama in the complexities of modern building technology has been Helmut Jahn's specialty. His seventeen-story atrium in the State of Illinois Center provides a new architectural sensation—an interior with the soaring effects of a street lined with skyscrapers.

Xerox Centre, Dearborn and Monroe streets. Completed 1980, C. F. Murphy Associates

Opposite: Xerox Centre was one of Helmut Jahn's first urban triumphs. He tailored a high-rise office building to fit its corner site rather than imposing a massive structure overwhelming everything else around it.

Above: Xerox Centre lobby. Jahn designed this building toward the beginning of a career that would grow increasingly outlandish, whimsical, and individualistic.

and imposing, he quickly established a national reputation. His work was successful with developers who were hungry for trademark buildings, and he attracted more than his share of the capital being spent in the real estate boom of the eighties. Jahn also cultivated an image of an architectural superstar: his photogenic wardrobe of capes and hats became well known. We learned much about his personal style, down to the kind of pen he used (Mont Blanc), and even the color of ink (sepia). Jahn became a target for jealous detractors, but in an age when individualism was celebrated, Helmut Jahn's buildings are nothing if not individualistic.

It is the view of many who know him that after the debacle of the State of Illinois Center, Jahn landed on his feet with the United Airlines Terminal at O'Hare Airport. This design also drew flak when it was built in 1987, mostly because it differed markedly from the calm Miesian terminals of the rest of O'Hare. But United was quickly appreciated for being both dramatic and simple. Like most Jahn buildings, this one is structural and modern, but its form harks back clearly to something historic. Its lofty and exposed superstructure represents a throwback to the great railroad sheds of the nineteenth century, Europe's early pavilions of steel and glass. Jahn's design seems to long for a time when travel was exciting and romantic.

Mies might well approve of the purity of the United building, with vast spaces framed entirely in white-painted steel. Yet it is decorative in a way that Mies never was, not only like the rail sheds but also like the Crystal Palace in Paris, or Chicago's own Rookery. As a whole, the building testifies to Jahn's self-described skill as a "synthesizer." He blends notes of the old with entirely modern techniques of construction. He designs in glass and steel as would the most relentless modernist, yet he finds ways to make the most basic steel beams and girders decorative. Those who resist using the term postmodernist to describe Jahn probably come closer to the mark when they call him a "romantic modernist."

THE LIBRARY COMPETITION

In 1988, when a jury of eleven awarded the design of Chicago's new main public library to architect Thomas Beeby, there was a collective sigh of relief. It came from the city's Library Board, which, to its growing embarrassment, had been without a central library for twelve years. The sigh came from the architectural community, which dislikes competitions and found this one particularly odious. It even came from the public, which was getting restless over what had become a protracted public drama.

The choice of Beeby's historically eclectic entry was by far the safest among the five finalists. This, of course, invited comparisons to the Tribune Tower competition held more than sixty years before. Beeby's "is a gentle building," a member of the jury stated when the library decision was announced. "It's beautiful. This looks like a library. This is a building that you can trust." The design, a combination of beaux-arts classical, Richardsonian Romanesque, and a number of other styles from Chicago's past, clearly struck the jury as the most agreeable. There had been enough architectural controversy, most memorably over Jahn's State of Illinois Center. "Trust" was the operative word in the jury's decision.

Opposite: United Airlines Terminal, O'Hare International Airport. Completed 1987, Murphy/Jahn
The terminal reveals a lofty steel superstructure meant to resemble that of an old railroad shed and imparts a sense that travel is still romantic and exciting. A unique essay by Helmut Jahn, it also salutes the architectural triumphs of the past. The great spaces of Chicago's past are evident. So are the precise compositions of glass and steel created by Mies van der Rohe. While Jahn has clearly survived the postmodern movement, the term "romantic modernist" suits his often successful combination of structuralism and whimsy.

The story of the Harold Washington Library Center goes back to 1976, when it was decided that the old library, designed by Shepley, Rutan and Coolidge and dedicated in 1897, was too small, and its books were moved to a warehouse on the Chicago River. This would be their temporary home while a new building was designed and constructed, quickly it was hoped. After an initial delay, planners for the new library focused on an old building, the former Goldbatt's store on State Street. Rehabbing this century-old structure seemed like the practical yet creative solution. Too many architecturally significant buildings had been torn down in Chicago of late. Goldblatt's was empty, and it was a fine example of the Chicago School by Holabird and Roche. Several years passed while studies were made. Then a strangely ferocious campaign by the *Chicago Sun-Times* against Goldblatt's upended it. A great city should have a great *new* public library, it was decided.

Cautious politicians caused additional delays. Finally in 1986 a vacant lot was chosen and the competition announced, at which point the Library Board made it clear they were impatient to get started. For that reason they shaped their competition around a "design/build" format. This meant that architects would enter as parts of teams that also were to include developers, engineers, and contractors. Each team would present its proposal and guarantee the $130 million price. While it sounds reasonable, the approach horrified many architects, and for good reasons. Such a system, for one, required a large investment by any competitor to just guarantee the eventual cost, so only wealthy and well-connected firms would be able to enter. The

Chicago Public Library competition entries, 1988

Above: Lohan Associates
The Lohan entry in the library competition was regarded by many as the most "Chicago" of the styles entered. It was to be steel and glass with a spacious and light-filled atrium running through the interior.

Opposite, above: Murphy/Jahn
Helmut Jahn's entry was typically radical, in search of a new definition of what is beautiful. After his controversial State of Illinois Center, Jahn had little chance of being selected for a commission that had generated ample controversy before the competition even began.

Center: Skidmore, Owings and Merrill
The SOM entry was a conservative postmodern approach to the new library. It lost because it seemed to lack innovation; neither did it stir the public's yearning for Chicago's noble past.

Below: Arthur Erickson
Erickson was the only out-of-town architect to enter. His proposal for a massive concrete building won significant public approval but was dismissed as something out of "Star Wars" by some members of the architectural establishment.

Harold Washington Library Center, State Street and Congress Parkway. Completed 1992, Hammond Beeby & Babka

Above: Thomas Beeby's winning design *looked* like a library to the members of the jury. It also looked like Chicago, albeit in conglomerate form, with notes of the Chicago School, the Columbian Exposition, and even Mies van der Rohe all folded into one building.

Below: The "winter garden" of the Harold Washington Library Center, a spectacular atrium, recalls the light courts of Chicago's past. But this one is on the top floor of the building where few use it, not at ground level where everyone must pass.

process also had the effect of removing the client, in this case the city, from any substantial creative role in the design. In fact, guidelines were preordained well before any architect put pencil to paper. Design teams had to sift through a thicket of detailed and relatively unalterable specifications, ranging from divisions of space to lighting and security requirements. When the competition was announced, one of the strongest objections came from the local chapter of the American Institute of Architects, which stated that working at arm's length with the client would not result in the best possible building.

Of the five entries submitted to the jury, each had merit, and when the models were put on public display, they provoked spirited, if inconclusive, debate. Among the proposed libraries, that of Dirk Lohan Associates was perhaps the most "Chicago" of the designs—a light-filled glass and steel box with a large atrium and grand staircase. That of Helmut Jahn was predictably radical; he assembled geometric shapes with his customary whimsy. Skidmore, Owings and Merrill submitted a mildly postmodern version of a Chicago School office block. Canadian Arthur Erickson submitted a huge concrete structure with rounded shapes so distinct that some dismissed it as a set from *Star Wars*.

Beeby's design, clearly the most conservative entry, looks back postmodernistically to Sullivan's Auditorium, just two blocks away, with thick granite walls and large Romanesque arches. Saluting the 1893 World's Columbian Exposition, which Sullivan so deplored, Beeby blends in some pediments and swags that recall the fair's extravagant classical style. Curiously, the back wall of the nine-story building is a glass curtain, a recognition of the city's Miesian past. Beeby's library is an ironic mix of styles, irony being a frequent postmodern trait: three thick masonry walls appear to bear the building's load, until the sheer glass of the fourth reveals that the walls are all a facade. Yet the message of the building is clear. Chicago's buildings did not evolve logically or in a straight line. Its architectural character is a blend of fragments guided by an intuitive hand.

Because it is a harmonious combination of fragments, the library is an attractive building. It is disappointing, however, because the idea that motivated Beeby on the exterior fails to penetrate the surface. Perhaps this was predictable, given the complex requirements of the project, but the spaces inside, from the entryway through most other public areas, are unremarkable. The only real exception is something called a "winter garden" on the top floor. Bathed in light and richly detailed, it suggests a Rookery-like atrium and has the vastness of universal space. But it is separated from the natural human flow of the library and is usually empty. Perhaps this is another hint of irony: the library's most striking public space is hidden in the attic.

CONSERVATISM VERSUS TRADITION

Chicago's library competition demonstrated, like the Tribune Tower competition before it, that conservatism in architecture is different from tradition. Conservatism leads to safe, if ultimately unsatisfying, choices. The architectural tradition of Chicago, on the other hand, has a long list of innovative buildings. Conservatism tends toward sentimentality. Tradition discovers new powers in the lessons of the past. By these standards, Beeby's library is conservative. Its creativity is superficial.

Reasserting traditional values in architecture is not always simple, however, because those values run deep and can cause much debate. In Chicago such a debate flared up in a pair of architectural exhibitions mounted in 1976, and they are still remembered as important events in recent Chicago architecture. The first of the exhibitions was entitled

"100 Years of Architecture in Chicago: Continuity of Structure and Form," which came to Chicago from Munich, where curators at Die Neue Sammlung museum attempted what they regarded as the broadest survey of Chicago architecture ever. Its thesis was that direct lines of influence tied the steel skeletons of William Le Baron Jenney to the towers of Mies van der Rohe. Chicago architectural tradition was expressed as simplicity, practicality, and form that follows structure.

As the German exhibition was scheduled to open at Chicago's Museum of Contemporary Art, a number of Chicagoans dissented. It cast Chicago tradition in far too narrow terms, they said, and as a result a local group of architects organized a counter-exhibition that included many Chicago architects of the past who had been left out of the show at the MCA. The counter-exhibition, called "Chicago Architects," was curated by Chicago architects Stuart Cohen and Stanley Tigerman, who were themselves searching for alternatives to pure modernism in their own work. The show included the work of Hugh Garden, Howard Van Doren Shaw, the Kecks, Andrew Rebori, and others. It also included the city's beaux-arts past, such as the Palace of Fine Arts at the 1893 Columbian Exposition, as prominent in Chicago history as it was unloved by structural purists. "Chicago Architects" made a mark. It showed that a true Chicago tradition went beyond buildings with big shoulders. Organic architecture in Chicago has been practiced in a variety of styles, utilitarian as well as romantic.

Chicago's blend of pragmatism and romance continues to manifest itself in its most successful buildings today. Dirk Lohan's Oceanarium at the Shedd Aquarium, for example, is a graceful addition to the original Shedd, a classical design by Graham, Anderson, Probst and White. Yet the new building also goes far beyond the dark interior of the old one. Outside, the Oceanarium is a curved marble structure with definite classical overtones. Inside is a striking universal space with a great glass wall separating the dolphin pool from a panorama of Lake Michigan. Lohan, who is the grandson of Mies van der Rohe, combines varied elements of Chicago tradition with a light but certain touch. And if the postmodern world calls for a twist of irony, the lakefront pavilion encloses a wooded habitat meant to resemble a shoreline in the Pacific Northwest.

In other examples of recent Chicago architecture, designs that appear whimsical also include a strong note of practical modernism. One such interior is The Painted Apartment, located in the Mies van der Rohe building at 2400 North Lakeview, overlooking Lincoln Park. The apartment was designed in 1983 by the firm of Krueck and Olson. Ronald Krueck, who earned his degree from IIT in 1970, says that the sensations of weightlessness and transparency that he finds in Mies's interiors were what inspired this one.

The Painted Apartment began as a fantasy of the client, who told Krueck that she could not afford the modern paintings that she liked so she wanted to "live inside one." Krueck created the space for this client with such high-tech materials as perforated metal and glass-block walls. They are supplies that might otherwise function in a factory, but they provide the space with an elegant sense of openness. Light penetrates and plays on surfaces in a variety of ways, often changing with the time of day, giving the apartment its richness and comfort.

The most important Chicago architecture of the present time demonstrates that architects can respond directly to traditional values and still discover innovative new forms. One Chicago building that has done this is 333 West Wacker Drive, a green glass tower that sits neatly on a narrow site at a bend in the Chicago River. The building, by the New York firm of Kohn Pedersen Fox, drew much praise for its simplicity and originality when it was built in 1983, yet its shape quickly confounded interior

Private Residence, Glencoe. Completed 1991, Larson Associates Inc.

Above left: The living room of this home overlooking Lake Michigan offers luxury in rich furnishings and a sense of expansive space in its height and its glass.

Above right: Repetition of basic form creates a harmonius and well-lighted master bathroom.

Lower left: The media room features a succession of distinct and uncomplicated images.

Lower right: Costly materials and flowing space contribute to a comforting kitchen.

John G. Shedd Aquarium (Oceanarium addition), 1200 South Lake Shore Drive. Completed 1991, Lohan Associates

Dirk Lohan's Oceanarium harmonizes beautifully with the old aquarium, though the addition is entirely different in concept. The old classical structure by Graham, Anderson, Probst and White is windowless and dark inside, creating a dramatic effect with the illuminated fish tanks. The new addition is bright with natural light pouring in from a glass curtain wall overlooking the lake. In many ways, the Oceanarium demonstrates the power and freedom of contemporary architecture. Although the Oceanarium is actually on a Great Lake, it is a convincing replica of an ocean bay in the Pacific Northwest, complete with sea mammals.

The Painted Apartment, 2400 North Lakeview Drive. Completed 1981, Krueck and Olsen

It looks anything but Miesian, but architect Ron Krueck, a graduate of IIT, took his lessons from Mies van der Rohe in combining basic materials with grace and care. Using industrial-grade metals and glass, the result is a refined dwelling wherein divisions of space are only suggested. The design satisfied the client's wish not to hang paintings but to live inside one.

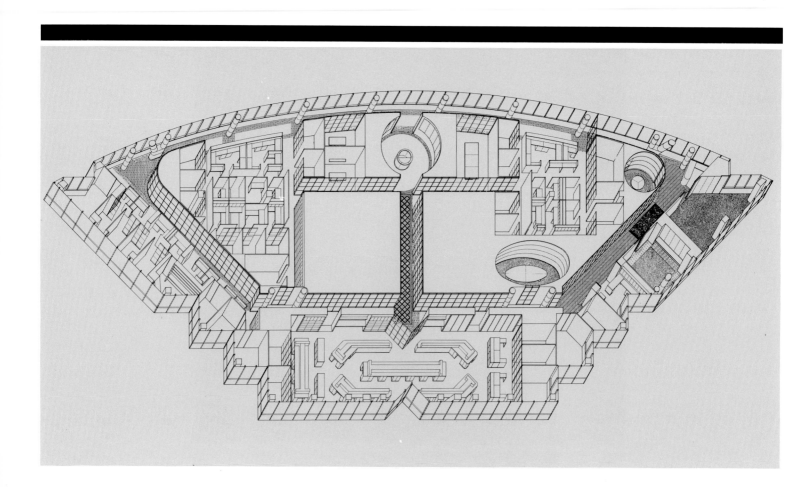

333 West Wacker Drive. Completed 1983, Kohn Pedersen Fox

Opposite and following pages: The postmodern world has become more curvilinear than the modernist one, and sometimes for the most rational reasons. The 333 office tower fits snugly into an odd-shaped piece of property at a bend in the Chicago River. Because it uses architectural imagery in subtle ways, it has been heralded as one of the best buildings of the eighties in Chicago. Its curtain wall is almost sheer and reflects sizable portions of skyline from a variety of angles. But mullions and spandrels show up in a slightly different in color—suggesting floors, offices, and real life inside.

Above: The floor plate demanded a unique approach to the interior—a corridor along the building's outside edge.

Above and below: 333 West Wacker Drive
The lobby of 333 West Wacker is small in scale but dramatic as it integrates the curves and transparency of the exterior.

Grace Episcopal Church, 637 South Dearborn Street. Completed 1985, Booth/Hansen
A large, open loft (with a crucifix showing up as part of the structure) became one of Chicago's most original church spaces created by architect Laurence Booth. Much as a mere sofa or rug can give an old warehouse residential character, Booth applied touches of ecclesiastical architecture to create a sacred space. Where printing presses once clattered, it is now quiet and engenders a sense of solemnity and well being.

---

designers. Some suggested the building was not as useful inside as it was appealing outside. What the design required, however, was a slightly different approach to space planning. A central corridor through each floor does not work well; it wastes space on either end of the crescent-shaped floor plan. Then it was discovered that placing the corridor to one side, along the exterior curve of the building, provided the space, light, and natural flow that Chicago architects have sought from the time of John Root onward. The lesson was that a unique conception for the exterior of 333 West Wacker demanded an equally new approach for the interior as well.

THE PROMISE OF PRESERVATION

It is natural that a city with Chicago's architectural tradition should have a strong movement in architectural preservation. Attention to the past in Chicago goes beyond the superficial interest of postmodernism. Rather, preservation in Chicago touches the most basic lessons of architecture: "form follows function," as Sullivan said, and "God is in the details," which was attributed to Mies.

It is ironic perhaps, but no contradiction that one of Chicago's most important preservationists is anything but a quaint antiquarian. He is a working architect who was trained as a Miesian, and a portion of his practice is the design of frankly modern houses. John Vinci graduated from IIT in 1960, yet while he was studying the essence of glass and steel, he also got involved in efforts to salvage decorative architectural detail from the Louis Sullivan houses that were coming down at the time with disturbing regularity. The exercise represented more than antique hunting by an architecture student. Vinci explains that it taught volumes about how detail contributes to the overall effect of a building's design. Sullivan's work is uncommonly rich in this respect, and the process of removing wood carvings from stairways and plaster panels from walls taught Vinci how materials, structure, and decoration could be integrated harmoniously and in meaningful ways.

Vinci's career as a salvager continued after college. He was hired to join a team to remove ornament and copy stencil designs from Sullivan's Garrick Theater, ticketed for demolition after one of the first legal battles ever in an attempt to save a building. Before the building came down, Vinci and a few colleagues cut away large sections of plaster ornament, exterior terra cotta, and other details, many of which were then distributed to museums around the country. It expanded appreciation for Sullivan, and for Vinci it reinforced the idea that the essence of architecture was borne out in sometimes small and subtle ways.

The preservation movement was still too weak in 1971 to preserve Adler and Sullivan's Stock Exchange on LaSalle Street, one of Sullivan's finest office buildings in Chicago. A move to save the building failed, but the protests of historians and preservationists were successful in extracting money from the developer for a similar salvage operation. A curator from the Art Institute, David Hanks, who was leading this effort, went to Vinci to discuss the project. Vinci made an unexpected suggestion—that they work not on scattered details but concentrate instead on a single space in the old building. "I thought it was important to see how many architectural details came together in a complete space," Vinci said. They chose the old Trading Room—which by then had a dropped ceiling covering art glass, paint over old stencils, and other alterations that disguised any former charm. Practicing his own kind of "architectural archeology," he recovered plaster ornament, cast-iron mullions, stencils on canvas wall coverings, and a variety of other Sullivan details. Also using old photos, a detailed conception of the once-glorious space emerged.

Two things happened next. First, one of Vinci's fellow salvagers, a photographer named Richard Nickel, was killed while trying to pull some last pieces of ornament from other spaces in the Stock Exchange. This was in April 1972, when Vinci's formal project was finished, but Nickel had an informal truce with the wreckers to allow him to get in with crow bar and hammer. As the structure was being readied for final demolition, Nickel climbed in one too many times, and a large section of the building collapsed on him. He was not found for several days. If there was a shred of consolation in this story it is that headlines of the tragedy highlighted the passion that many felt for old buildings.

About a year later another set of events was moving forward. The new wing of the Art Institute was in the final design stages, and curators of the museum were reportedly dissatisfied with the predictable modern design of the new place, an addition to the elegant classical style of the museum's main building on Michigan Avenue. Instead of resigning themselves to another modernist box, however, the Art Institute made a novel proposal. The old Trading Room—partially saved and fully documented—could be re-created in the large reception room of the new wing. Money was quickly raised, and Vinci and his partner, Lawrence Kenny, were hired. Over a period of a year they re-created stencils, recast plaster ornaments, reset skylights, and reproduced furniture (some of it based on the photographs). The result of this consummate attention to detail is a total effect that appears extraordinarily true to a Sullivanesque interior. Though it is a massive room, it is delicately wrought and filled with gentle light. Often abuzz with activity, it can instill calm. Faithful to Sullivan, form follows function. The remarkable thing is that its function—as an aesthetic experience as well as a place to buy and sell securities—is so marvelously conceived.

Chicago Stock Exchange Trading Room, East Wing of the Art Institute of Chicago. Originally completed in 1894 by Adler and Sullivan, reconstructed in 1977 by Vinci-Kenny Architects
The Trading Room was filled with ornament but remained reposed and organized, a tribute to Sullivan's genius. It was saved through the efforts of a band of dedicated preservationists, including architect John Vinci, Chicago's leading architectural "archeologist."

Chicago Stock Exchange Trading Room

For Sullivan, "form follows function" was anything but a simple dictum. In stenciling the reconstructed Trading Room, sixty-five shades of green, red, blue, and gold were used. The patterns are almost mind-boggling in their complexity, but like a plant with branches, leaves, and flowers, all the parts of Sullivan's imagery connect. The effect, therefore, is organic unity in a huge interior space.

The success of the Trading Room did not have the immediate effect of saving all old buildings from destruction, but it had an impact. Beginning with the recession of the seventies and continuing in the building boom of the eighties, a number of important buildings were preserved and restored—some at great expense and most with all due attention to detail. The Rookery, the Monadnock Building, the Railway Exchange Building, the old Chicago Public Library (now Cultural Center), and the Printer's Row loft district just south of the Loop were beneficiaries of a growing appreciation for history and of a growing group of architects skilled at restoration.

These projects and others like them show that the lessons of preservation and restoration are immense. They teach, for one, that Chicago architects were truly three-dimensional designers, and impressive exteriors often grew out of practical and well-thought-out interiors. They also teach that the most marvelous spaces can be fashioned of the most modest materials. Sullivan did with plaster, paint, wrought iron, and colored glass what other architects fail to achieve with far more expensive materials.

Most important, old buildings in Chicago demonstrate that many basic values in architecture do not change. As the objectives of economy, natural light, and simplicity have served Chicago architects for over a century, they also serve the most important architects of today. As time passed, these values penetrated deeply into the Chicago architectural tradition. They evolved dramatically with the influx of architects after the Great Chicago Fire and continued with each generation responding in their own ways. Today the historical terrain is rich with insight to solve new architectural problems as they arise.

Chicago became and has remained the center of American architecture because of this underlying power. Its tradition testifies that a building can be utilitarian or wildly romantic, it can be a skyscraper or a bungalow, but the crucial elements of any architecture are things that are not immediately obvious. In Chicago they include sensations of space, a fascination with materials, and a conviction that buildings can elevate the spirit.

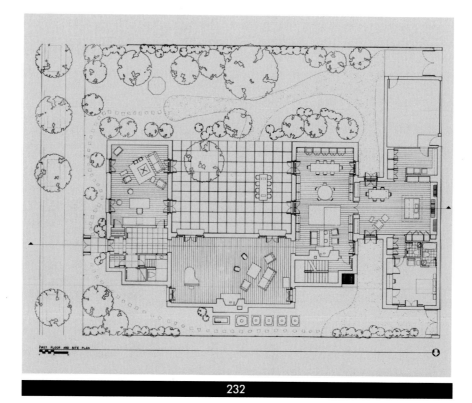

FIRST FLOOR AND SITE PLAN

Manilow House, Chicago. Completed 1991, Max Gordon with John Vinci

Above: The late English architect Max Gordon designed this house as a home and gallery for a major collector of art. The exterior is reminiscent of early German houses designed by Mies before World War II. As was true with Mies, the simplicity of the overall design provides a setting for fine-crafted finishes and large-scale art.

Opposite: Floor plan of the Manilow house.

Manilow House

Above: An Anselm Kiefer canvas (right), period furniture, and lineal steel-frame window system combine harmoniously in the living room.
Opposite, above: The gallery/exhibition space has a large peaked skylight.
Below: John Vinci, Gordon's Chicago-based associate, designed the many details of the house and kitchen, which are minimalist and functional in nature but wrought of rich materials and classical proportions.

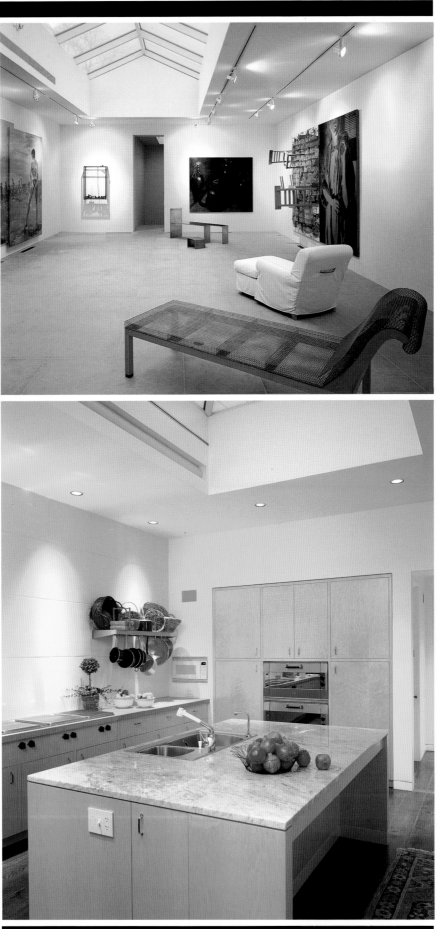

GLOSSARY

ART DECO

The term came from the Exposition Internationale des Art Decoratifs et Industriels Modernes in Paris in 1925, which lionized streamlined and geometric design in metals, glass, and other materials of the mass-produced world. Art Deco, or Art Moderne, also refers to buildings, mostly skyscrapers, constructed in the thirties that were stripped down and emphatically modern.

ARTS AND CRAFTS MOVEMENT

Englishman William Morris began the movement in the mid-1880s with design that depended on handcrafts and eschewed machine-made techniques. Regarded as morally uplifting, arts and crafts reflected truth in materials and craftsmanship and led to a fashion for carved wood, painted tiles, wrought iron, and medieval images. American arts and crafts, advanced by Frank Lloyd Wright, among others, at the turn of the century, was more conspicuously modern but retained the same fascination with materials such as wood, brick, and glass.

BEAUX-ARTS

Beaux-arts is the style of architecture named after the Ecole des Beaux-Arts in Paris, where many American architects trained in the later 1800s. The Ecole was considered up-to-date in that it taught the "primacy of the plan"—that interior space must be laid out before exterior decoration can be designed. But it was traditional and antimodern in that it called for strict use of classical forms.

CENTURY OF PROGRESS

The second great world's fair in Chicago, the Century of Progress took place in 1933 and 1934. Architecturally, it was noted for streamlined modernism and foreshadowed the design of houses and buildings in the latter half of the twentieth century. Showcased at this world's fair was the House of Tomorrow designed by George Fred Keck. It was largely prefabricated and featured walls of glass, air conditioning, metal-tube furniture, and a hangar for an airplane on the ground floor.

CHICAGO LOOP

Chicago's downtown was (and is) called the "Loop" since the time streetcars formed a ring around the central business district. The Loop was bordered on three sides by water (the Chicago River on the north and west; Lake Michigan on the east), which made property therein dear and led to the need for taller buildings in Chicago.

CHICAGO PLAN

Daniel Burnham's city plan for Chicago was published in 1909. It depicted a parklike setting much influenced by the great cities of Europe. Burnham's plan was never entirely realized, but it encouraged Chicago architects toward openness and great size in the manner of the 1893 World's Columbian Exposition, which was directed by Burnham. It also pushed architects toward classicism and away from an indigenous style of Chicago's own.

CHICAGO SCHOOL OF ARCHITECTURE

The term refers to the commercial architects of the late 1800s who dedicated themselves to office and loft buildings of the simplest possible design. Exteriors did little to conceal the steel-frame

Opposite: 860–880 North Lake Shore Drive

cage that was their interior support system. These buildings have been admired for their truthfulness and "structuralism"—they are what they seem—and they represent a truly indigenous American architecture.

THE CLIFF-DWELLERS

By Henry Blake Fuller, this novel was one of the nation's best-sellers of the 1890s. Set in Chicago, the action takes place in a skyscraper, a vivid symbol of power and ambition that existed everywhere but particularly in this bustling and sometimes frightful center of commerce and industry.

ILLINOIS INSTITUTE OF TECHNOLOGY

Ludwig Mies van der Rohe came to Chicago in 1937 to take over the architecture department at the Armour Institute of Technology. The school's name was soon changed to Illinois Institute of Technology, and it moved to a new campus designed entirely by Mies. IIT grew to become world famous as a mecca of modern architecture and design.

INTERNATIONALISM

Starting in the thirties, important ideas in modern architecture were advanced at the Bauhaus, a school of design in prewar Germany directed by Walter Gropius and later by Mies van der Rohe. They advocated the use of machine-made materials such as metal and glass, powerful geometric forms, and utter rationality, as opposed to traditional styles. Internationalism was a term coined by the curators of an exhibition of European architecture in the thirties at New York's Museum of Modern Art. The International style drew little from any local context or heritage.

LIGHT WELL

Also known as a "light court," this is the open center of office buildings into which sunlight could pour and illuminate interior offices. Chicago architects were among the first to develop the idea of the light well, as the crowded downtown, the Loop, required all manner of strategies to bring maximum light inside. Oftentimes the first few stories of a light well were covered with glass ceilings, creating elegant atrium spaces in many buildings, most notably John Wellborn Root's Rookery.

MODERNISM

This term refers to the effort of artists in the late nineteenth and early twentieth centuries to take art beyond the idea of representational beauty and express underlying content. As part of the movement, modern architects developed entirely new forms to suit the latest building technologies and current lifestyles. William Le Baron Jenney's steel-frame buildings are considered modern. Louis Sullivan's organic architecture was modern, as were the flowing and open spaces of Frank Lloyd Wright. The International style of Mies van der Rohe reduced architecture to its most fundamental terms, after which the modern movement in architecture floundered and postmodernism made its appearance.

ORGANIC ARCHITECTURE

Architecture is organic to the extent that it corresponds to the forms and forces of nature. A house that blends with the natural beauty of its site is considered organic. Organic architecture, which became an obsession for Louis Sullivan and second nature to Frank Lloyd Wright, came to mean architectural form that is deeply suited to its use.

POSTMODERNISM

The postmodern movement began as a rejection of the minimalism and uniformity inherent in modernism. Beginning in the late 1960s, this meant a recovery of historic architectural forms in contemporary buildings—columns, arches, ornamentation—and a rejection of the "forced amnesia" that critics attributed to modern architecture. Ultimately, postmodernism led to caricature and excess, which resulted in the discrediting of the movement.

PRAIRIE SCHOOL

The Prairie School refers to the attempt to develop an indigenous architecture of the Midwest. Pioneered by Frank Lloyd Wright, the Prairie style reached its height through him and some of his close followers. Their residential designs were often low and long, reflecting the prairie horizon, and used such modest local materials as oak, brick, and handcrafted fixtures throughout.

RICHARDSONIAN "ROMANESQUE"

As American architects searched for forms that were characteristically American in spirit, Henry Hobson Richardson alighted on the Romanesque. Although originating in medieval Europe, the Romanesque was powerful and somewhat raw, like America itself. It was appreciated also because its piers and arches expressed structure rather than concealed it with classical ornament.

SEVEN LAMPS OF ARCHITECTURE

This book by English art critic and aesthete John Ruskin, first published in 1880, attempted to reduce the canons of architecture to seven "lamps," which included sacrifice, truth, power, beauty, life, memory, and obedience. It made arguable assumptions, such as the unsuitability of iron in buildings, but was read and otherwise absorbed by early modern architects in Chicago.

SKYSCRAPER

In nineteenth-century Chicago, any building over ten or eleven stories high was regarded as a skyscraper, a building type made possible through the development of steel-frame construction. William Le Baron Jenney's ten-story Home Insurance Building in the Loop was one of the world's first such buildings. The one hundred and ten-story Sears Tower, two blocks from the site of the now-demolished Home Insurance, is currently the tallest in the world.

TRIBUNE TOWER COMPETITION

In 1922, the *Chicago Tribune* held a design competition for a new office tower on Michigan Avenue. The newspaper selected a neo-Gothic skyscraper, which was built the following year, but the second-place entry by Eliel Saarinen of Finland drew the most critical praise for its sleek lines and powerful skyward thrust. Saarinen's never-built tower inspired a new generation of modern commercial buildings in Chicago and elsewhere. It also prompted Saarinen to move to the United States, where he was thrust into the limelight as an important modernist architect.

UNIVERSAL SPACE

Mies van der Rohe attempted to create large spaces unencumbered by bearing walls. This enabled the most flexible use by the occupants; it was also a welcomed architectural challenge. As Mies succeeded in creating these spaces in buildings such as Crown Hall at the Illinois Institute of Technology, he enclosed them in glass, implying that such space extends to infinity and is indeed "universal."

WORLD'S COLUMBIAN EXPOSITION

Chicago's 1893 world's fair was then the largest event of its kind, exhibiting the arts, sciences, technologies, and other trappings of civilized modernity. Architecturally, however, it was a reversion to the past, a beaux-arts extravaganza that was utterly and perfectly classical in style. The fair gave Chicago a patina of Europe that was much enjoyed, but it ended the local fashion for the simple but elegant buildings of the indigenous, structuralist Chicago School of architecture.

Blaser, Werner. *Mies van der Rohe: Furniture and Interiors*. Woodbury, New York: Barron's, 1982.

Brooks, H. Allen. *The Prairie School: Frank Lloyd Wright and his Midwest Contemporaries*. Toronto: University of Toronto Press, 1972.

Bruegmann, Robert. *Holabird & Roche, Holabird & Root: An Illustrated Catalogue of Works*. 3 vols. New York and London: Garland Publishing, 1991.

Callahan, Carol J. "Glessner House, Chicago, Illinois," *The Magazine Antiques* 139 (May 1991): 970–81.

Chappell, Sally Anderson. *Architecture and Planning of Graham, Anderson, Probst and White, 1912–1936: Transforming Tradition*. Chicago: University of Chicago Press, 1992.

Cohen, Stuart E. *Chicago Architects*. Catalogue for an exhibition organized by Laurence Booth, Stuart E. Cohen, Stanley Tigerman, and Benjamin Weese. Chicago: Swallow Press, 1976.

Condit, Carl W. *The Rise of the Skyscraper*. Chicago: University of Chicago Press, 1952.

Cowles, Linn Ann. *An Index and Guide to An Autobiography, the 1943 Edition by Frank Lloyd Wright*. Hopkins, Minnesota: Greenwich Design, 1976.

Dart, Susan. *Edward Dart: Architect*. Unpublished manuscript. Lake Forest, Ill: 1992.

Drexler, Arthur. *Ludwig Mies van der Rohe*. London: Mayflower Publishing Company; New York: George Braziller, Inc., 1960.

Eaton, Leonard K. *Two Chicago Architects and Their Clients: Frank Lloyd Wright and Howard Van Doren Shaw*. Cambridge: MIT Press, 1969.

Garrigan, Kristine Ottesen. *Ruskin On Architecture*. Madison: University of Wisconsin Press, 1973.

Giedion, Sigfried. *Space, Time and Architecture: The Growth of a New Tradition*. Cambridge: Harvard University Press, 1941.

Gill, Brendan. *Many Masks: A Life of Frank Lloyd Wright*. New York: G. P. Putnam's Sons, 1987.

Glibota, Ante and Frederic Edelmann. *Chicago: 150 Years of Architecture, 1833–1983*. Paris: Paris Art Center and L'Institut Français d'Architecture, 1983.

Goldsmith, Myron. *Myron Goldsmith: Buildings and Concepts*. New York: Rizzoli, 1987.

Hitchcock, Henry-Russell. *The Architecture of H. H. Richardson and His Times*. New York: Museum of Modern Art, 1936; Cambridge: M.I.T. Press, 1966.

Hoffmann, Donald. *The Architecture of John Wellborn Root*. Baltimore: Johns Hopkins University Press, 1973.

Hubka, Thomas C. "H. H. Richardson's Glessner House: A Garden in the Machine." *Winterthur Portfolio* 24 (Winter 1989): 209–29.

Joediche, Joachim. *Helmut Jahn: Design of a New Architecture*. New York: Nichols Publishing Company, 1987.

Jordy, William H., and Ralph Coe, eds. *American Architecture and Other Writings by Montgomery Schuyler*. 2 vols. Cambridge: Harvard University Press, Belknap Press, 1961.

Lynes, Russell. *The Tastemakers*. New York: Harper & Brothers, 1954.

Menocal, Narciso G. *Keck & Keck: Architects*. Madison: University of Wisconsin, 1980. Catalogue for an exhibition at the Elvehjem Museum of Art.

Monroe, Harriet. *John Wellborn Root*. Boston and New York: Houghton, Mifflin & Company, 1896.

Morrison, Hugh. *Louis Sullivan: Prophet of Modern Architecture*. New York: W. W. Norton, 1935.

Mumford, Lewis. *Roots of Contemporary American Architecture*. New York: Reinhold Publishing, 1952. New York: Dover Publications, 1972.

O'Gorman, James F. *H. H. Richardson: Architectural Forms for an American Society*. Chicago: University of Chicago Press, 1987.

————. *H. H. Richardson and His Office*. Cambridge: Department of Printing and Graphic Arts, Harvard College Library, 1974.

Pratt, Richard. *David Adler*. New York: M. Evans and Company; New York: J. B. Lippincott 1970.

Ragon, Michel. *Goldberg On the City*. Paris: Paris Art Center, 1985.

Ruskin, John. *The Seven Lamps of Architecture*. Sunnyside, Orpington, Kent: George Allen, 1880; New York: Dover Publications, 1989.

Russell, Frank, ed. *Mies van der Rohe: European Works*. London: Academy Editions; New York: St. Martin's Press, 1986.

Schipporeit, George, project director. *Mies van der Rohe: Architect as Educator*. Chicago: Illinois Institute of Technology, 1986. Catalogue for an exhibition of the Mies van der Rohe Centennial Project.

Schulze, Franz. *Mies van der Rohe: A Critical Biography*. Chicago: University of Chicago Press, 1985.

Slavin, Maeve. *Davis Allen: Forty Years of Interior Design at Skidmore, Owings and Merrill*. New York: Rizzoli, 1990.

Tafel, Edgar. *Years with Frank Lloyd Wright: Apprentice to Genius*. New York: Dover Publications, 1979.

Twombly, Robert C. *Louis Sullivan: His Life and Work*. New York: Viking, Elisabeth Sifton Books, 1986.

————. *Louis Sullivan: The Public Papers*. Chicago: University of Chicago Press, 1988.

de Wit, Wim, ed. *Louis Sullivan: The Function of Ornament*. New York: W. W. Norton, 1986. Catalogue for an exhibition organized by the Chicago Historical Society and the St. Louis Art Museum.

Wright, Frank Lloyd. *An Autobiography*. New York: Duell, Sloan and Pearce, 1943; New York: Horizon Press, 1977.

Zukowsky, John, ed. *Chicago Architecture, 1872–1922: Birth of a Metropolis*. Munich: Prestel-Verlag, 1987. Catalogue for an exhibition at the Art Institute of Chicago.

Since 1968 the Commission on Chicago Landmarks has designated important works of architecture as historic landmarks. Listed below is a selection of these sites, some of which are open to the public. For information on these and other buildings, the Landmarks Preservation Council, the Chicago Architecture Foundation, and the Commission on Chicago Landmarks are among useful resources.

JANE ADDAMS' HULL-HOUSE AND
DINING HALL
800 South Halsted Street
Main house, 1856; dining hall, Pond and
Pond, 1905

ALTA VISTA TERRACE DISTRICT
One-block street at 3000 north
and 1050 west
Row houses developed by Samuel
Eberly Gross
1900–1904

ASTOR STREET DISTRICT
Astor Street between North Avenue and
Division Street
From 1880

AUDITORIUM BUILDING
430 South Michigan Avenue
Adler and Sullivan
1889

EMIL BACH HOUSE
7415 North Sheridan Road
Frank Lloyd Wright
1915

CARSON PIRIE SCOTT AND COMPANY
BUILDING
1 South State Street
Louis Sullivan
1899 and 1904 with a 1906 addition by
D. H. Burnham and Company

JAMES CHARNLEY HOUSE
1365 North Astor Street
Adler and Sullivan, Frank Lloyd Wright
1892

CHICAGO BOARD OF TRADE BUILDING
141 West Jackson Boulevard
Holabird and Root
1930

CHICAGO PUBLIC LIBRARY CULTURAL
CENTER
78 East Washington Street
Shepley, Rutan and Coolidge
1897

CITY HALL/COUNTY BUILDING
Bounded by LaSalle, Clark, Randolph, and
Washington streets
Holabird and Roche
1911

FINE ARTS BUILDING
410 South Michigan Avenue
Solon S. Beman
1885

FISHER BUILDING
343 South Dearborn Street
Charles Atwood of D. H. Burnham and
Company
1896 with a 1907 addition

GETTY TOMB
Graceland Cemetery
Louis Sullivan
1890

JOHN J. GLESSNER HOUSE
1800 South Prairie Avenue
Henry Hobson Richardson
1887

WALTER BURLEY GRIFFIN PLACE DISTRICT
Griffin Place between Wood Street and
Prospect Avenue
1910–14

ISIDORE H. HELLER HOUSE
5132 South Woodlawn Avenue
Frank Lloyd Wright
1897

HOLY TRINITY ORTHODOX CATHEDRAL
AND RECTORY
1121 North Leavitt Street
Louis Sullivan
1903

HUTCHINSON STREET DISTRICT
Off Marine Drive at 4232 north
George Maher
1894–1914

IMMACULATA HIGH SCHOOL
Irving Park Road and Marine Drive
Barry Byrne
1922

JEWELERS' BUILDING
15–17 South Wabash Avenue
Adler and Sullivan
1882

K.A.M. SYNAGOGUE
1100 East Hyde Park Boulevard
Alfred S. Alschuler
1924

SIDNEY A. KENT HOUSE
2944 South Michigan Avenue
Burnham and Root
1892

KRAUSE MUSIC STORE
4611 North Lincoln Avenue
Louis Sullivan
1924

ALBERT F. MADLENER HOUSE
4 West Burton Place
Hugh Garden and Richard Schmidt
1902

MANHATTAN BUILDING
431 South Dearborn Street
William L. Jenney
1891

MARQUETTE BUILDING
140 South Dearborn Street
Holabird and Roche
1894

MONADNOCK BLOCK
53 West Jackson Boulevard
Burnham and Root, 1891; Holabird and
Roche, 1893

NAVY PIER
Grand Avenue and Lake Michigan
Charles S. Frost
1916

OLD WATER TOWER
Chicago and Michigan avenues
W. W. Boyington
1869

OLD COLONY BUILDING
407 South Dearborn Street
Holabird and Roche
1894

PILGRIM BAPTIST CHURCH
3301 South Indiana Avenue
Adler and Sullivan
1891

PRAIRIE AVENUE HISTORIC DISTRICT
Prairie Avenue between 18th Street and
Cullerton Avenue
1870–1900

RELIANCE BUILDING
32 North State Street
D. H. Burnham and Company
1894

FREDERICK C. ROBIE HOUSE
5757 Woodlawn Avenue
Frank Lloyd Wright
1909

ROOKERY BUILDING
209 South LaSalle Street
Burnham and Root
1886

SECOND PRESBYTERIAN CHURCH
1936 South Michigan Avenue
Exterior: James Renwick, 1874;
interior renovation: Howard Van Doren
Shaw, 1900

JOSEPH JACOB WALSER HOUSE
42 North Central Avenue
Frank Lloyd Wright
1909

THREE ARTS CLUB
1300 North Dearborn Street
Holabird and Roche
1914

TRIBUNE TOWER
435 North Michigan Avenue
Hood and Howells
1925

INDEX

Page numbers in *italic* refer to illustrations.

H

I

J

K

L

M

N

O

P

Q

R

S

T

U

V

W

X

Z